"*Better Than Brunch* is a fascinating study of the church growing in 'the carcass of Christendom' in Cascadia. Byassee and Lockhart tell these stories masterfully so we all can learn how to redescribe church for the new world coming. A surprising book packed with much inspiration. Read it and learn mission all over again."

—David Fitch, Lindner Chair of Evangelical Theology, Northern Seminary, and author of *Faithful Presence*

"Here's a little book that is sure to have a big impact. Two of our best-connected theologians and experienced practitioners of the church's mission—Ross Lockhart and Jason Byasee—together give us the theological rationale and the practical, encouraging examples we need to be a more faithfully missional church. *Better Than Brunch* (what a great title!) views the future through the lens of some of the most creative and faithful congregations of Cascadia to provide the rest of us just the boost we need to better work with Christ in leading Christ's mission to his world."

—Will Willimon, Professor of Christian Ministry, Duke Divinity School, and author of *Who Lynched Willie Earle? Preaching to Confront Racism*

"It is the cardinal rule for good writing: don't tell, show. In this excellent piece of work the authors do just that. They show us churches and church leaders who are embodying a new way of being church for a new time. Of particular value is the book's focus on the Cascadia region of the northwest US and British Columbia. Christendom never had quite the foothold in Cascadia as it did in the east and midwest. While many have lamented that, Byassee and Lockhart see the opportunity in it."

—Anthony B. Robinson, author *Transforming Congregational Culture and Changing the Conversation: A Third Way for Congregations and Their Leaders*

"In *Better Than Brunch*, Byassee and Lockhart share the treasures they discovered in interviews and site visits with church leaders and congregations in Cascadia. These treasures took the form of eight patterns, all of which are relevant to anyone in church leadership in Cascadia. Particularly helpful were the questions at the end of each chapter that congregations can use to begin their own treasure hunt as they seek to strengthen their ability to be healthy, faithful, and effective local Christian communities. I recommend the use of the book as a part of a facilitated process in churches that want to do a thorough examination of their common life and purpose."

—MELISSA M. SKELTON, Archbishop of the Diocese of New Westminster, Metropolitan of the Ecclesiastical Province of BC and Yukon

"My friends Ross and Jason have written a troubling but encouraging book. Troubling because they expose the reality of where we live. With their flare for engaging, lively, punchy rhetoric, they take us into the post-Christendom mind—and lived experience—of the majority of those living in Cascadia, what one pastor they interview has dubbed 'the carcass of Christendom,' a world devoid of any living memory of the gospel, suffering the social and relational consequences of the deprivation, but hungering for the love of the Jesus they are about to encounter through his disciples. Or, are supposed to encounter. But encouraging. Ross and Jason set out on 'a treasure hunt' where I live and serve, as 'detectives of divinity,' as Alan Roxburgh calls them, looking for 'clues of the Triune God' at work where supposedly such a God is not. And find them in eleven churches, each embodying eight elements of authentic mission with Jesus. You may not agree with every expression of mission they call 'divine,' but they challenge us, me, to look beyond the facades to the redeeming work of the risen Jesus. Read and be troubled by how many of us have bought into 'Christendom metrics' for forming and evaluating ministry, and be encouraged by the stunning signs of 'kingdom metrics' abounding on the West Coast of North America."

—DARRELL JOHNSON, Teaching Fellow, Regent College

"In *Better Than Brunch*, Jason and Ross articulate the unique grip that secular culture has over the Pacific Northwest and the challenges churches face. But far from merely naming the problem, they offer fresh solutions. Their compelling thesis that missional and unapologetically evangelical churches are the answer challenges both progressives and evangelicals alike. This makes the book relevant not just to their geographical context but across North America."

—MATT MIOFSKY, Lead Pastor of The Gathering United Methodist Church, Saint Louis, Missouri

"*Better Than Brunch* is better than a safari. Keep your hands in the vehicle as you ride through this wild kingdom known as Cascadia, the most secular corner in all of North America. In a region strewn with carcasses of Christendom, you'll encounter the wild fauna who have evolved to thrive: a Korean-American 'OG womanist' who preaches like an African-American while wearing a Black Lives Matter T-shirt; an LGBTQ+-inclusive Methodist pastor who isn't above carrying someone else's inconsolable child on her hip while she preaches; a pastor who has lived with thirty-eight people, often with very different last names and socioeconomic backgrounds; my own sibling, Ken Shigematsu, who I thought I knew, but it turns out I don't; plus, churches that aren't defending their space, but giving it away to build affordable housing; a church with no sign out front; another with a tent city ensconced on its lawn, and now counts its occupants as members. *Better Than Brunch* is a thrilling encounter with a new generation of insurgent pastors who reject the usual yardsticks of what successful churches look like. Instead, they are fostering communities built on the kind of radical inclusivity and social justice Jesus himself would recognize."

—TETSURO SHIGEMATSU, playwright, author, and broadcaster

"*Better Than Brunch* offers a candid depiction of the church's missional context in Cascadia, which stretches from Oregon through Canada's British Columbia. In this mossy context, Christians exist on the margins of influence, and yet Jason Byassee and Ross Lockhart show that when the gospel is assimilated from the margins, it can spark a missional imagination that invites the center to give Jesus a second (or first) look!"

—TRYGVE D. JOHNSON, Hinga-Boersma Dean of the Chapel, Hope College

Better Than Brunch

Better Than Brunch

Missional Churches in Cascadia

Jason Byassee
and Ross A. Lockhart

Foreword by Darrell L. Guder

CASCADE *Books* • Eugene, Oregon

BETTER THAN BRUNCH
Missional Churches in Cascadia

Cascade Books
An Imprint of Wipf and Stock Publishers
199 W. 8th Ave., Suite 3
Eugene, OR 97401

www.wipfandstock.com

PAPERBACK ISBN: 978-1-7252-8117-2
HARDCOVER ISBN: 978-1-7252-8118-9
EBOOK ISBN: 978-1-7252-8119-6

Cataloguing-in-Publication data:

Names: Byassee, Jason, author. | Lockhart, Ross A., author. | Guder,
Darrell L., 1939–, foreword.

Title: Better than brunch : missional churches in Cascadia / Jason
Byassee and Ross A. Lockhart ; foreword by Darrell L. Guder.

Description: Eugene, OR : Cascade Books, 2020 | Includes
bibliographical references.

Identifiers: ISBN 978-1-7252-8117-2 (paperback) | ISBN 978-1-7252-
8118-9 (hardcover) | ISBN 978-1-7252-8119-6 (ebook)

Subjects: LCSH: Case studies. | Missions—North America. | Christian
leadership. | Twenty-first century. | Mission of the church—United
States. | Christian leadership—United States. | Mission of the church—
Canada. | Christian leadership—Canada. | Christianity—21st century.

Classification: BV2070 .B93 2020 (paperback) | BV2070 .B93 (ebook)

12/18/20

For Wade and Vern,
who taught me about friendship, and so about church
—J. B.

For Richard Topping,
colleague, friend, and catalyzer of missional imagination
—R. A. L.

Contents

Foreword

There are many reasons to include a foreword by another author in a newly appearing book. In the case of this volume, Jason Byassee and Ross Lockhart invited me to write a foreword for *Better Than Brunch* in order to locate their work in a missiological conversation in which I have been involved, and which is ongoing. I am honored and delighted to be invited to write this foreword and look forward to the appearance of *Better Than Brunch*, and to the discussion that it is certain to foster.

In their introductory explanation of the investigations that generated *Better Than Brunch*, Byassee and Lockhart analyze the distinctive secularization of the cultures of "Cascadia" (Oregon, Washington, and British Columbia). How the Christian mission should address these secularized cultures is the concern that drives their argument. In that analysis they are drawing on the "Gospel and Culture" discussion that emerged in the 1980s in Britain and North America. In 1984, noted ecumenicist and missiologist (and "retired" missionary) Lesslie Newbigin energized the British engagement with late Western Christendom as a mission field with his booklet entitled *The Other Side of 1984: Questions for the Churches*. Under his encouragement, the conversation crossed the Atlantic and began to develop momentum in North America. An informal network began to grapple with Newbigin's challenge to explore how faithful Christian witness was to take place in the secularized cultures of late Western Christendom on both sides of the North Atlantic. It's at this point that our stories begin to merge.

Under the auspices of the emerging Gospel and Our Culture Network (GOCN), George Hunsberger and Craig van Gelder published a first collection of essays in 1996 with Eerdmans entitled *The Church Between Gospel and Culture: The Emerging Mission in North America*. These papers were written for and debated in regular gatherings of the growing GOCN. It then succeeded in getting a grant to pursue the following question: If the cultural context of Western Christendom is rapidly becoming a secularized mission field, what kind of theological work must be done if the church is to understand itself and function within our cultures as a missionary movement? To put it more technically, how does Western Christendom do ecclesiology with God's mission as the driving theme? Or, as phrased in *Missional Church*: "What would an understanding of the church (an ecclesiology) look like if it were truly missional in design and definition?"[1] To explore the many dimensions of that query, a team of six missiologists was recruited to spend three years researching this challenge. It was funded by a grant to the Network for this purpose. The team worked through the contemporary literature on the general subject and developed an outline of themes and sub-themes that needed to be addressed. It consolidated its findings in chapter themes and ultimately generated a multi-author volume that hoped to function as the stimulus for the formulation of a missio-centric doctrine of the church.

The group entitled the resulting book *Missional Church: A Vision for the Sending of the Church in North America*.[2] We (naively) hoped that, as those who coined the term, we could define it for the ensuing discussion. The point was to put mission at the defining

1. Guder, *Missional Church*, 7.

2. Guder, *Missional Church*, See the bibliography in this volume which documents the rapid expansion and diversification of the "missional church discussion." With the publication in 1996 of *The Church Between Gospel and Culture* and in 1998 of *Missional Church*, the Eerdmans Publishing Company initiated the "Gospel and Our Culture Series," which continued under the aegis of the GOCN until the mid 2020s, when the Network quietly restructured itself as the Forum on Missional Hermeneutics which meets at the Society for Biblical Literature every year.

center of our theologizing about the church's purpose and actions. The discussion took off immediately and the book evoked a lively debate that, to our surprise, rapidly became both ecumenical and international. The term "missional" was adopted but was quickly laden with an enormous spectrum of definitions and nuances rendering it virtually unusable. It was an overnight cliché. It was my privilege to serve as the coordinator of the three-year study project that generated *Missional Church,* to write three chapters for it, and to edit the published volume.

In the lively discussion that ensued, there was a constant reiteration of concern about the shape and practice of a "missional church." What did it look like? Are there examples one can look at? Can it to be reproduced? This led the GOCN to initiate a second research project (with a second grant!). This project was coordinated by Lois Barrett, who had been one of the six researchers on the *Missional Church* team. It was the task of the two coordinator/editors to ensure that a multi-author volume would cohere and make its case with clarity. The second round of work generated a second book in 2004 with Lois Barrett as editor entitled *Treasure in Clay Jars: Patterns in Missional Faithfulness.* It is this second volume that Jason and Ross have chosen as a resource for their exploration of mission in post-Christendom Cascadia. There are some fascinating divergencies between this project's approach and emphases and the findings discussed in *Treasure in Clay Jars.* But, at the level of foundational claims, there is a remarkable consensus. In her introductory chapter for *Treasure in Clay Jars,* Lois Barrett formulated a theological consensus that captured the shared convictions of both research teams. The implied question to which she is responding could be formulated as follows: What is theologically distinctive about a "missional" church or congregation? What are the theological criteria for a "missional church"?

A missional church is a church that is shaped by participating in God's mission, which is to set things right in a broken, sinful world, to redeem it, and to restore it to what God has always intended for the world. Missional churches see themselves not so much sending as being sent.

A missional congregation lets God's mission permeate everything the congregation does—from worship to witness to training members for discipleship. It bridges the gap between outreach and congregational life, since, in its life together, the church is to embody God's mission. These basic assumptions are also affirmed by Byassee and Lockhart in their introduction to the book you are about to read.

The discussion documented by *Treasure in Clay Jars* went through several tactical stages to accomplish its task. We started by attempting to frame "empirical indicators" of a missional community. In the discussion of "method" at the end of *Treasure in Clay Jars* these indicators were laid out with attempts to describe what they actually look like in the practice of a "missional community." The language of "indicators" gave way to "patterns," which proved a more constructive while modest approach. Ultimately, *Treasure in Clay Jars* became a book that described and interpreted the congregation using the eight "patterns" of missional theology and practice. The patterns were first used to identify congregations across North America that presented themselves as evidencing missional ferment and innovation. Then, in teams of two, we conducted intensive visits with nine selected communities, testing how the patterns actually worked (one of the nine churches selected was a network of seven Reformed Church in America congregations in New Jersey). The chapters we wrote summarized our findings by expounding the patterns that demonstrated missional theology and practice and using our congregations as the evidence or examples. Although *Treasure in Clay Jars* did not create a public response as large and diverse as did *Missional Church*, the list of patterns did re-surface frequently as a workable outline for diverse approaches to defining a "missional church." And it has obviously proven useful to Byassee and Lockhart in their provocative analysis of "mission, meaning, and motivation in the Pacific Northwest."

The strategy adopted by Byassee and Lockhart moved beyond *Treasure in Clay Jars* in order to generate its own catalogue of "elements or patterns." These emerged from their intensive conversations with a very diverse range of communities in Cascadia. Rather than using their "elements" to select the churches they would investigate, they selected churches based upon personal experience and collegial recommendations. They then distilled their list of analytical categories from intensive conversations with the leaders of these congregations. The outcome is a fascinating mosaic of very distinctive churches that documents just how challenging post-Christendom Cascadia has become. The authors document their credentials as highly insightful readers of Cascadian culture by the skillful ways in which they describe and analyze the cultural and theological challenges they were investigating. I find considerable overlap in the content of the two lists, which I read as a validation of the work done by both teams. But at the same time, much that I read in *Better Than Brunch* is a learning experience, so much so that I am frequently grateful for the authors' expositions and interpretations. They are leading me into new pastures!

Better Than Brunch does, in fact, move the missional-theological discussion into uncharted waters with some of the patterns it adds to the list as well as the communities it investigates. Deeply appreciative of their prodding us forward, I want to commend to their readers two themes which, in my mind, represent bold advances in the discussion (I could have chosen several more, but there are limits to the amount of space a lowly foreword may claim). The second chapter, entitled "Progressive and Evangelical: A Necessary Paradox," unpacks a bold critique of the division of the Christian movement into right-wing/evangelical/conservative camps versus left-wing/progressive/modernist wings. The authors of *Better Than Brunch* unpack their critique by describing several large churches in Vancouver that defy that stereotypical divisiveness. They grapple with issues that never arise in many congregations, and they actively look for ways to demonstrate to their watching world that the gospel crosses chasms of division and builds bridges that humans look upon as impossible.

The divided Christian movement is a sad reality that challenges the fundamental understanding of the church as God's missionary people. It makes coherent Christian witness before an unbelieving world virtually impossible and undermines any credibility that Christianity may still have. The modern Ecumenical Movement was a response to the appeal from the younger churches that the divisions of the churches of Western Christendom, who were sending out their missionaries to the younger churches, made their Christian witness untenable. The *Better Than Brunch* churches take up theological and moral issues that are important, even threatening, because they must be addressed if gospel witness is to be faithful and believable. But how that is done is the crucial question. The gospel is not a message of peace if its witnesses are constantly engaged in mutual judgmentalism and hostility. Christians who are forgiven sinners will always have matters about which they disagree. But a divided and divisive community is by definition disobedient. *Better Than Brunch* frames the overcoming of such Christian divisiveness as a fundamental first step for missional integrity today.

The question of the "How" of Christian corporate witness is addressed by *Better Than Brunch* under the rubric "Missional Metrics." At the end of each chapter, the authors raise questions for "Reflection and Action." The chapter on "missional metrics" asks, "How do you and your community measure effectiveness in ministry?" The language may be a little startling. In the discussion of the missional church there is a constant criticism of the market mentality that dominates the American church's understandings of success. But *Better Than Brunch* makes a compelling point: it is important to track effectiveness. The issue is the criteria of effectiveness. Rather than adapting ourselves to the marketplace definition of success, which easily betrays the gospel, we are to develop transformed criteria that frame effectiveness in terms of integrity, mutual support, and clear articulation of the gospel. A missional metric is one of the outcomes of the biblical formation of the witnessing community. It will replace marketplace success criteria with a focus upon Christlikeness linked with responsible stewardship of the gifts God gives to shape his people for their vocation as witnesses. As part of that process, it is going to be necessary to ask about "effectiveness." And it is going to be necessary to scrutinize the ways our communities interact with each other to determine how faithful we are to the calling to be communities of growing love.

While the *Treasure in Clay Jars* team was working through the various stages of its studies, we came to the shared conviction that our entire process could be understood as a response to Paul's formation of the Corinthian community in 2 Corinthians 4. We found for each of the patterns a biblical statement that illumined the practice of the pattern. The outcome of the entire process was the shared confidence expressed by the apostle: "So we do not lose heart"[3]—especially when we consider the end of Christendom that surrounds us. We learned with the Corinthian community that "we have this treasure in clay jars so that it may be made clear that this extraordinary power belongs to God and does not come from us."[4] We found it liberating to understand ourselves as modest and limited "clay jars," whom God is shaping as instruments of his healing purposes for the whole world. Given this biblical shaping of the entire clay jars project, it is interesting to note that the GOCN has generated a steadily expanding interrogation of what we now call "missional hermeneutics." Growing numbers of colleagues are grappling with various aspects of the fundamental claim that the purpose of the biblical witness is the continuing formation of witnessing communities, wherever God has sent them.

The focus of *Treasure in Clay Jars* and before it *Missional Church* has been to serve God's mission by rediscovering the vocation of witness of the gathered, equipped, and sent community. We are profoundly grateful that our original intention to stimulate theological processes that center on the discovery of and submission to our missional vocation is being met and serendipitously expanded and deepened. *Better Than Brunch* is a particularly gratifying serendipity. It is a surprise and a delight to expand and enrich the missional enterprise by discovering the treasure chests and treasure maps in Cascadia. These discoveries reveal gospel treasures that equip clay-jar Christians for their service.

DARRELL L. GUDER
Professor of Missional and Ecumenical Theology Emeritus
Princeton Theological Seminary

---

3. 2 Cor 4:1, 16.

4. 2 Cor 4:7.

Acknowledgments

A s pastors and theological educators, we are deeply grateful for all the vibrant and inspiring relational connections God has given us here in the Pacific Northwest these past many years. We are blessed daily through the conversations and curiosities of our fellow faculty, staff and students at The Vancouver School of Theology (VST). In particular, the visionary leadership of St. Andrew's Hall professor and VST Principal Richard Topping has created an environment for thoughtful, engaged, and generous Christian leadership that, in his words, helps us go "deep with God and wide with the world."

This project was based in The Centre for Missional Leadership (CML) at St. Andrew's Hall, and we are grateful for our colleagues in the Centre including Senior Fellow Darrell Guder and CML associates Andrea Perrett and Tim Dickau. Funding for this project was made possible through the generous support of British Columbia Synod's "Presbyterian Innovative Ministries" of The Presbyterian Church in Canada. We are grateful for their support and encouragement, including from David Jennings as Convenor. This project would not have been possible without the inspiring Christian leaders in the region who so generously gave of their time from filling out surveys, in-depth interviews, welcoming us into their worshiping communities, and taking many, many follow-up questions.

Acknowledgments

We are grateful for the time and wisdom of our interview subjects, of which this book is the fruit. We were not able to use all of their insight, obviously, but we delighted in all of their company and grew throughout our time together. We hope they recognize themselves faithfully portrayed here, even if they do not agree with all of our conclusions.

Finally, we thank our families for their enduring patience, endless humor, and quick provision for our humility when needed on a regular basis. To Jaylynn, Jack, Sam, and Will, as well as Laura, Emily, Jack and Sadie, we offer our love and thanks.

Introduction

Treasure Chest

In the summer of 2019, an organization called *Gold Hunt* buried a treasure chest resembling something from the set of a pirate movie, filled with twenty gold and eight hundred silver pieces worth one hundred thousand dollars somewhere in the Greater Vancouver area. Participants could purchase a map for thirty-five dollars or upgrade to a map with some clues for fifty-five dollars. Part murder mystery, part Amazing Race reality show, this geo-caching game included a video-based storyline and invited people to form teams to fan out across the city solving riddles in the hope of striking it rich.

Around the same time the authors of this book were involved in our own treasure hunt in the region. We've been on the lookout for clues of the Triune God's activity in the Pacific Northwest region of North America known as Cascadia. Cascadia is a geographic region running South to North following the outline of the Cascade mountains including the American states of Oregon and Washington as well as the Canadian province of British Columbia. Cascadia as a region has shared environmental, cultural, economic, and political (even separatist!) shared values. People take this concept of Cascadia so seriously they've even made their own flag, known as the Cascadia Doug (named for the Douglas Fir tree), should these two states and one province ever decide to take this courtship to the next level.[1] Most importantly, this region is home to us. Not home by birth, but like many Cascadians it is home by choice. Some people *were* born in this Pacific Northwest paradise of soaring mountains, lush rainforest, and sparkling Pacific Ocean waves. The rest of us just got here as fast as we could!

As Christian pastors preaching Sunday-by-Sunday as well as seminary professors teaching weekly in the classroom, we're all too aware of something else that is special about this part of North America. It is also the most secular corner of the United States and Canada. People here sure love creation without paying much heed to the Creator. Secularism is not unique to this corner of the continent, of course, and much work has been done on documenting the decline of the mainline Protestant denominations in both countries since the mid-1960s. A recent study by two Canadian scholars, Stuart Macdonald and Brian Clarke, narrates the steps of mainline Christian denominational decline in the final decades of the last century right across the country. In *Leaving Christianity* Macdonald and Clarke describe the contemporary context this way:

> Decline in Christian affiliation, membership, and participation started in the 1960s and has picked up pace rapidly since then. This trend is likely to continue and, indeed, accelerate as an increasing portion of the country's population—among youth especially—have never been exposed to Christianity . . . In short, Canadian society is entering into a new era, a post-Christian era. The end of Christendom, we will argue, occurred in the closing decades of the twentieth century, as churches lost their social power and their place in the nation's cultural fabric.[2]

While secularism is being felt across the country, it is especially pronounced here on the West Coast. Census data on both sides of the border is clear that "no religion" is now the number one religion in the region.[3] Historian Tina Block's survey of faith in Cascadia found

1. See "Our Flag," https://cascadiaunderground.org/cascadia-underground/cascadia-doug-flag/.

2. Clarke and Macdonald, *Leaving Christianity*, 11.

3. Block, *Secular Northwest*, 2. In her scholarly treatment of religion in

that "Northwest secularity is most evident in the region's strikingly low levels of involvement in, and attachment to, formal or organized religion."[4] Some believe that the quick pace of that unraveling in Oregon, Washington State, and British Columbia is due, in part, to the reality that Christendom was never fully established here compared to back east. Historian Lynne Marks pushes hard against even the classic secularization theory (or perhaps we might borrow Charles Taylor's subtraction theory here) being applied to British Columbia noting "to become secularized, a culture must first be religious. Was this ever true of settler British Columbia?"[5] Whether living on the secular west coast or sniffing a scent of the fumes of Christendom in eastern Canada, the landscape of Christian witness has changed for (formerly) mainline Protestant churches as one scholar remarked, "Canadian culture holds a hermeneutics of suspicion regarding the church."[6]

We were speaking to an experienced church-planter friend of ours in Portland recently. She commented on how she loves to go to local coffee shops with her husband and play "spot the new church planter from Christendom Texas." Having been a church planter herself, she knows what to look for. "There they are," she joked, "skinny jeans and flannel shirt, along with ironic facial hair and a full sleeve of tattoos. Sitting there just sipping their coffee, working on their laptop and scheming on how to start a church. What they don't get is that the soil is different here in Cascadia. This is a church-planting graveyard if you don't come prepared." But here's the thing, there is *treasure* to be found in the soil here. We were sure of it. That's why we wrote this book. Like the treasure hunters searching for a chest full of valuable coins, we wanted to search for clues, chase down leads, talk to people and prayerfully reflect on what God is up to in this beautiful and rugged landscape.

Cascadia, Block argues that historically, "Northwesterners were part of a regional culture that placed relatively little importance on formal religious connections."

4. Block, *Secular Northwest*, 48.

5. Marks, *Infidels and the Damn Churches*, 11.

6. Goertz, "Toward a Missional Theology of Worship," in *Between the Lectern and Pulpit*, 167.

As Vancouver missiologist Alan Roxburgh describes this kind of work, we were being "detectives of divinity." In many ways, both the decline of traditional, mainline Christianity in the Pacific Northwest as well as a fascinating array of new missional communities in the ruins of Christendom, make the limited scope of Cascadia the perfect "ecclesiastical petri dish" for those anywhere across North America interested in what Christian community will look like in the years ahead. Christendom: that fifteen-hundred-plus-year experiment of the church's privileged place in Western society, including access to political power and possessing cultural cache. Beginning in the fourth century and going through a series of corrections from the Enlightenment on, the end of this special status for the church could be sensed with more of a whimper than a bang in the closing decades of the last century.

For those who had eyes to see and ears to hear, the end of Christendom prompted a deep and honest reflection on the reductionisms that were required to have the gospel of the risen Lord Jesus fit into a Latin Western European belief system of State Churches. As early as 1932 theologian Karl Barth was arguing for a greater emphasis upon the missionary vocation of the church and the missionary nature of the Triune God that David Bosch later described as changing from a "church centred mission . . . to a mission centred church."[7] English-born, Church of Scotland–sent missionary Lesslie Newbigin moved to India in 1936 in the classic Christendom mode of mission, a well-educated Westerner sent to teach the gospel in a foreign land. By all accounts, Newbigin did well in this model and helped form the Church of South India as an independent denomination by the time he left. Returning to England in 1974, however, Newbigin was shocked at the shift over several decades having left a nominally Christian Britain only to return and find it secularized. Newbigin formed the Gospel and Our Culture Network and began asking questions of Christian witness and mission using the missionary skill set he honed overseas. Newbigin's missiological questions were noticed in North America and his lectures at Princeton Theological Seminary, later published as

---

7. Guder, "From Mission and Theology to Missional Theology," 43.

Foolishness to the Greeks, challenged the North American audience of scholars and ministry practitioners to consider whether the West could be converted from its growing secularity. His central question, "What would be involved in a genuine missionary encounter between the gospel and the culture which is shared by the peoples of Europe and North America and their colonial and cultural offshoots, the growing company of educated leaders in all the cities of the world, the culture with which those of us who share in it usually describe as modern?"[8]

Church leaders in North America took up the challenge and Darrell Guder convened a research group of missiologists in the 1990s, through the Gospel and Our Culture Network, to examine the nature of mission in an increasingly post-Christendom Canadian and American context. The result of that original consultation and subsequent research by Guder and his colleagues was the publication in 1998 of *Missional Church: A Vision of the Sending of the Church in North America*. The book proved to be a groundbreaking project that shaped the conversation on missiology not only in North America, but surprisingly to the team themselves, also around the world. Today, *Missional Church* continues to be in demand in print, pulpit, and classroom translated into different languages, as a basic text on understanding the shifting nature of Christian witness in a post-Christendom world.

Immediately upon publication of *Missional Church*, however, Darrell Guder and other authors were met with questions such as, "Where could one look to find a concrete example of a missional Christian community in North America?" and "How would you know a missional church if you saw one?" They heard from church leaders who were wondering, "How can our congregation find enough encouragement to continue to move toward becoming missional?" In response, a number of *Missional Church* authors engaged in another research project, this time visiting, interviewing, and profiling examples of missional Christian witnessing communities across North America. They selected Paul's encouraging words to the house church(es) in Corinth as their guiding text: "Therefore,

---

8. Newbigin, "Theory of Cross-Cultural Mission," 3:51—4:20.

since through God's mercy we have this ministry, we do not lose heart . . . but we have this treasure in jars of clay to show that this all-surpassing power is from God and not from us."[9]

The six authors became "treasure hunters" criss-crossing North America looking for clues of God's activity giving shape to missional communities. In a Luke 10 approach, they were sent out in pairs to visit different sites identified through their networks as missional in nature. However, we imagine they did not follow Luke 10's instructions literally and most certainly took carry-on bags, and if not a purse then most definitely a credit card! They established the following threefold criteria for a missional church:

1. A missional church is a church that is shaped by participating in God's mission, which is to set things right in a broken, sinful world, to redeem it, and to restore it to what God has always intended for the world.

2. Missional churches see themselves not so much sending, as being sent.

3. A missional congregation lets God's mission permeate everything the congregation does—from worship to witness to training members for discipleship. It bridges the gap between outreach and congregational life, since, in its life together, the church is to embody God's mission.[10]

The pairs visited churches in such diverse locations as Colorado, Wisconsin, Washington State, Michigan, New Jersey, New York, Montana, California, and Ontario, Canada. Lois Barrett served as editor on the project and from the examples gathered of missional communities, the team identified "patterns of missional faithfulness" common to all as follows:

Pattern 1: Discerning Missional Vocation

The congregation is discovering together the missional vocation of the community. It is beginning to redefine "success" and "vitality"

9. 2 Cor 4:1, 7.

10. Barrett, *Treasure in Clay Jars*, x.

in terms of faithfulness to God's calling and sending. It is seeking to discern God's specific missional vocation ("charisms") for the entire community and for all of its members.

Pattern 2: Biblical Formation and Discipleship

The missional church is a community in which all members are involved in learning what it means to be disciples of Jesus. The Bible is normative in the life of the church's life. Biblical formation and discipling are essential for members of the congregation.

Pattern 3: Taking Risks as a Contrast Community

The missional church is learning to take risks for the sake of the gospel. It understands itself as different from the world because of its participation in the life, death, and resurrection of its Lord. It is raising questions, often threatening ones, about the church's cultural captivity, and it is grappling with the ethical and structural implications of its missional vocation. It is learning to deal with internal and external resistance.

Pattern 4: Practices That Demonstrate God's Intent for the World

The pattern of the church's life as community is a demonstration of what God intends for the life of the whole world. The practices of the church embody mutual care, reconciliation, loving account-ability, and hospitality. A missional church is indicated by how Christians behave toward one another.

Pattern 5: The Public Witness of Worship

Worship is the central act by which the community celebrates with joy and thanksgiving both God's presence and God's promised future. Flowing out of its worship, the community has a vital public witness.

Pattern 6: Dependence on the Holy Spirit

The missional community confesses its dependence upon the Holy Spirit, shown in particular in its practices of corporate prayer.

Pattern 7: Pointing Toward the Reign of God

The missional church understands its calling as witness to the gospel of the inbreaking reign of God, and strives to be an instrument, agent, and sign of that reign. As it makes its witness through its identity, activity, and communication, it is keenly aware of the provisional character of all that it is and does. It points toward the reign of God that God will certainly bring about, but knows that its own response is incomplete, and that its own conversion is a continuing necessity.

Pattern 8: Missional Authority

The Holy Spirit gives the missional church a community of persons who, in a variety of ways and with a diversity of functional roles and titles, together practice the missional authority that cultivates within the community the discernment of missional vocation and is intentional about the practices that embed that vocation in the community's life.

While the book set out to accomplish its goal of highlighting a missional church in order to encourage other Christian communities into missional practice, *Treasure in Clay Jars* never received the acclaim of *Missional Church* nor had the same kind of perceived impact. Nevertheless, for many of us who read the book when it was first published, there was a clear sense of missiologists attempting to narrate where the missional "rubber hit the road." Over the last twenty years there has been an explosion of publications, seminars, and consulting firms cashing in on the concept of "missional," so much so that some of the original authors of *Missional Church* are wary of using the term "missional" at all today. And yet, the same questions that prompted the publication of *Treasure in Clay Jars* are still being asked in Christian communities in search of their own gospel treasure in an even more secularized landscape.

With this in mind the community of scholars associated with The Centre for Missional Leadership at St. Andrew's Hall began to wonder what it might mean to ask similar questions posed by *Treasure in Clay Jars* but set within the narrower regional context of Cascadia. As the Senior Fellow in Residence for The Centre for Missional Leadership, Darrell Guder helped narrate the steps of how *Missional Church* and *Treasure in Clay Jars* developed, as well as the intention behind both projects. Guder was always clear and careful, however, to never speak on behalf of any of the authors on either project, noting the diverse set of opinions and perspectives on both teams within the Gospel and Our Culture Network (GOCN). These two GOCN publications remain a fascinating blend of differing viewpoints from multiple, renowned missiologists examining communities of faith across North America in a diverse set of contexts. Our scope was more limited, and our process more fitted to the particularities of the Pacific Northwest alone. As a first step, Professors Ross Lockhart, Jason Byassee, and Darrell Guder hosted a Centre for Missional Leadership consultation over two days in May 2018, inviting a group of missionally-minded pastors from both sides of the border to St. Andrew's Hall, Vancouver, to explore the theme of missional churches in Cascadia. Together they shared their own experiences of Christian witness in the rocky soil of Cascadia, as we studied scripture and prayed together, listening carefully for the Holy Spirit. We also laughed a lot, enjoyed each other's company, and feasted on good food while sampling some of Vancouver's best craft beer. Coming out of the consultation, there was a renewed sense of the need for this project to move forward. Thanks to the generous support of the Presbyterian Innovative Ministries of British Columbia Synod, a research grant was secured, and the process began in earnest.

Using the threefold definition of a missional church in *Treasure in Clay Jars* referenced above, we worked through our contacts in the region for suggestions of churches that would be good places for us to visit and study in Oregon, Washington State, and British Columbia. From that point forward, however, we set aside the pressure to have our research and writing conform to the patterns and practice of those who authored *Treasure in Clay Jars*. We honored the spirit of their work by seeking out local Christian witnessing communities for evidence of missional engagement but did not feel called to fit Cascadian churches into the continent-wide discerned patterns developed over fifteen years earlier. Instead, we began our site visits in 2019 going into each community open-minded and ready to listen and learn from missional practitioners. By early 2020, and thankfully before COVID-19 shut down the possibility of field work, we had completed site visits at eleven churches of various denominational flavors ranging from Orthodox to free-church evangelical megachurches to small neighborhood mainline communities focused on social justice. Writing retreats on the beautiful Sunshine Coast and in Vancouver helped us discern common themes coming out of these diverse and seemingly divergent Christian communities in Cascadia. We are grateful for the time and treasure shared with us in person from the following communities: Agape Church, Annunciation Orthodox Church, Tualatin Presbyterian Church, and Portsmouth Union Church, Portland; Quest Church and Union Church, Seattle; Faith United Methodist Church, Issaquah; Tidelands Presbyterian Church, Stanwood; Grandview Church, Tenth Church, and Tapestry Church, Vancouver.

The patterns that emerged in our reflection on the site visits and interviews were not meant to mirror or enhance the original patterns developed fifteen years earlier in *Treasure in Clay Jars*. Instead, we felt free to follow the treasure hunt wherever the clues directed us. And the churches we visited, diverse as they were, had certain patterns in common. We identified the following treasure map from our time roaming the Pacific Northwest, with diverse churches offering evidence of the following elements or patterns:

1. a sense of holy urgency that fuels entrepreneurial expressions of ecclesiology;
2. a fusion of evangelical and liberal theology;
3. a willingness to name, disempower, and turn away from sacred cows of tradition for the sake of partnering with what God is up to now;

4. missional leadership that is bold yet humble, shaped by the heart and mind of God;

5. churches crafted for the local context, free from competition and reflecting the unique characteristics, needs and gifts of a particular community;

6. metrics of effectiveness tied to the impact of God's love for neighbor rather than prestige or self-preservation;

7. deep formation through catechesis leading to thick community that no longer looks to the culture for help in making disciples; and

8. a hopeful, future-orientated faith that frees churches (and their leaders) from building ecclesiastical fiefdoms in the here and now.

The title of our book emerged as a surprise in the midst of our research. It came to us as a gift from the Holy Spirit when we were interviewing Ken Evers-Hood at Tualatin Presbyterian Church in suburban Portland. Reflecting on the high secularity in the region and the number of failing and mediocre churches, Ken reflected on how important creating a dynamic, arts-based, transformative worship service is. He said, "Look, if your Sunday morning service isn't better than brunch—you're screwed."[11] *Better than brunch.* We sure hope worshiping, serving, and delighting in God the Father, Son and Holy Spirit is better than brunch. Is that true of your local church? Would you like it to be? Well, across Cascadia we found evidence of Christian communities gathered by the Triune God, transformed through worship and service, deepening their discipleship, seeking justice, and participating in the reconciliation of broken lives and neighborhoods—a foretaste of the healing of the nations. In the end, our hunt led us to find some amazing communities full of grace and goodness—treasure just waiting to be found—full of something more precious than silver or gold: the grace and goodness of God.

11. Okay, so Ken used language stronger than "screwed." But if we used his preferred word choice, we might sell a few more copies in airport bookstores, but every last copy would be yanked by your friendly neighborhood Christian bookseller.

1

Holy Urgency and the Worship of the Triune God

In 1965, the Anglican Church of Canada did something that would be hard for any of our churches to conceive of doing today. They enlisted one of their country's best-known writers to do a report on the state of the church. Pierre Berton had sold millions of copies of books on Canadian history and culture, and now turned his formidable eye to the state of Anglicanism in the Dominion. His report was not complimentary. *The Comfortable Pew* compared the church to the passengers on a listless cruise ship.[1] Activities are announced, but the hearers are so bored they can make out no specifics. Are we going anywhere? I can't remember. Does it matter? And recall that this was the 1960s, the world was aflame with a hunger for social change. The only good news Berton could find was that the church was so irrelevant it could hardly be accused of holding back the tide.

Contrast this with the image of God's people in the Scriptures. In the book of Acts, God's people are blown by the hurricane-force gale of the Holy Spirit toward the four corners of the earth

1. Berton, *Comfortable Pew.*

(Acts 1:8). For example, Philip, with no warning, is commanded to go out to a wilderness road in the desert (Acts 8:26). There he meets an Ethiopian eunuch, servant of Candace, queen of the Ethiopians, riding in his chariot home from worshiping in the Jerusalem temple. Told to join the chariot, Philip *runs* (8:30). This is beyond odd. In our day, people run for fun. In the ancient world, you only ran if something was chasing you. Philip runs alongside a chariot and asks the eunuch what he is reading, presumably while moving his legs at chariot-speed. Thankfully he is invited in, sits, learns the eunuch is perplexed by the prophet Isaiah, and tells the man about Jesus, God's own suffering servant. When the eunuch spots water (in the desert?!), he exclaims, "Look, here is water, what is to prevent me from being baptized?" Nothing. Not his not being Jewish. Not his rich dark skin. Not his lack of sexual wholeness. Not his (former) lack of knowledge. Not even his wealth or power. So, *both* Philip *and* the eunuch dive down into the water for baptism (8:38). You can almost physically hear later Christians objecting, "wait, this isn't how we do things, he needs years of preparation, the pastor doesn't go down in the water too . . ." but before you can get the complaint voiced, the deed is done. Philip is "snatched" by the Spirit of God and finds himself hundreds of miles away, and the eunuch goes back to Africa, rejoicing. He is that continent's first convert, the one to whom hundreds of millions of African Christians today trace their spiritual descent. The story has not an ounce of fat on it, it is a blur, no time to lose.[2]

Contrast this with the last mainline Protestant worship service you attended, or even led. Did it feel like anything was at stake? Even if what the pastor was saying was true, would it matter? Did the timber of her voice suggest urgency? Could you imagine someone running to get in, so urgent was the subject matter?

Let us try another biblical example. Abraham is sitting by his tent in the heat of the day (Gen 18:1). And three strangers appear. Neglecting the temperature, and the ache in his ninety-year-old

2. I owe this telling to my colleague Mark Stein, who presented a paper on Jewish and Christian stories of running at VST's Interreligious Studies conference in spring of 2020. I so appreciate a Jewish interpreter of a New Testament passage! Mark also paired the story with Genesis 18.

bones, and his own dignity, Abraham *runs*, meets them, and bows to the ground (18:2). He offers them an underwhelming menu: a little water, a little bread, prison fare nearly (18:4–5). Then he proceeds to *run* again (18:6). Sarah must *quickly* make cakes. He *runs* to the herd to have a calf prepared (how long would slaughter-to-plate take?!). Then he presents his guests with a magnificent meal and stands while they eat (18:8). It is fit for kings. Not Jewish kings necessarily. This mixture of milk and meat is a clear violation of kosher laws. Lucky for Abraham, those laws have not yet been given to Moses. But later rabbis, out of their respect for the patriarchs, have to figure out how Abraham would have served a meal in violation of coming laws that he had to have intuited. Christians would come to see this as a glimpse of God the holy Trinity. These three are spoken of as one Lord (19:2). Jews speak of Abraham's extravagant hospitality to strangers. They announce God's plan to birth the family through which God will repair the world through Abraham and Sarah's barren marriage. Sarah laughs. Scripture does not here record Abraham's reaction. Perhaps by then he'd collapsed from all the running. He'd been in a hurry all day. And heard a world-saving word from the Lord for his efforts. Careful how you treat strangers: They just might be God.

Now for all this running by God's people—the evangelist Philip and the patriarch Abraham—we don't mean to suggest that *God* hurries. In fact, as anyone who has ever prayed for divine intervention knows, God can take his sweet time about things. This is a God who waited for the crown of creation, human beings, to evolve over millions, nay, billions of years. Christians think of the doctrine of the Trinity as our key belief, yet God waited for four centuries for us to work out the biblical math ourselves, rather than delivering it to us fully baked on a platter (to illustrate the time period, I sometimes ask churches what they were up to four hundred years ago, say, in 1620. See?). Fr. Matthew of Annunciation Orthodox Church outside Portland knows full well that sometimes the church errs in its teaching. But God will rehabilitate us out of that error. Might not be quick. Could take years, decades, or even, he says, a century or more. Don't worry. The Holy Spirit will press us to get the gospel that God wants. God never hurries.[3] God is patient. Jesus of Nazareth spent a mere thirty-year life among us.[4] For 90 percent of that life, we have no record of what he did. Went to synagogue. Helped his family. Prayed and fasted. One would think he had a world to save and ought to get to it. An eternal God will get the world God wants, short time or long.

But God's people are called to be about God's business of saving the world. There is not a moment to lose. St. Mark's favorite word in describing Jesus's ministry is "immediately." There is a cross to get to, a world to save. St. Paul is desperate to have a community witnessing to the resurrection in every part of the known world, so he is trying to get to Spain before the emperor's sword falls. These new covenant saints learn their zeal from Israel's history. David's downfall begins in the spring of the year, when kings go out to battle (2 Sam 11:1). David, instead, lounged. Rape and murder and ruin ensue. Other kings of Israel are evaluated on two things: do they allow false worship? The few good kings in Israel—Hezekiah, Josiah, Jehosophat—cut down the idolatrous poles in high places, and insist, in shrill and prophetic hoarse voices, that the God of Israel alone will be worshiped. And, good kings in Israel insist that justice will be done for the widow, the orphan, the stranger. These two—right worship and proper justice—are always twins. The kings learn this vital pairing from the Torah. Moses's laws combine an insistence on the oneness of God with a mandate to care for the vulnerable. No sooner than the laws come down the mountain and we, God's people, are defying both. Moses reacts with hot-blooded anger, breaks the tablets, melts the golden calves, grinds up their remains and makes us drink it. Many die, but the lesson is unforgettable. You eat, digest, and become what you worship. Moses trudges back up the mountain for more tablets. We human beings cannot live without a word from the Lord.

As leaders and observers of churches, we sometimes see this holy urgency more clearly outside the historic mainline. Evangelicals want to reach every person with the gospel. The joy of life in

3. Thinking here of Kelly Johnson's brilliant essay "God Does Not Hurry," in Laytham, *God Does Not . . .*, 63–82.

4. See Wells, *Nazareth Manifesto.*

God cannot be kept to themselves, it must be shared. So, they will adapt technology, shift once-cherished ways of worship, seek creative ways to invite or even disrupt—whatever it takes to reach the next person. Social-justice churches recognize that human beings cannot wait for the basic needs of life. Someone not housed or fed or otherwise in danger cannot be sent away and advised to come back tomorrow. The Black church in the US is used to being told that justice can wait. "These things take time," those in power say with a patronizing pat on the head. No. They cannot wait. Justice must happen now. Lives are at stake. Perhaps listlessness then is a product of Christendom, a sense that all is well with the world, why rush? That's the world Pierre Berton described so well. Evangelicals and social-justice advocates alike would insist that all is not right with the world. The gospel does not wait because lives are at stake.

Worship is urgent. These missional churches in Cascadia show that in their life together.

When Ken Shigematsu[5] arrived at Tenth Church in Vancouver, he was the congregation's twentieth pastor in twenty years. An administrative assistant pointed out the obvious—if the church closed on his watch, he would be blamed. As unfair as that would be, she was right. As a former corporate employee, Ken did what he knew how to do. He threw his whole self into the job. He worked long hours, he shifted worship around, he survived a coup attempt and the departure of long-time leaders and givers, by sheer force of will he turned the ship around.

He does not advise pastoring this way, mind you.[6]

Ken is a master of spinning the mythology of Tenth. He never tires of telling his key stories. His staff teases him for this. One skit at an anniversary celebration of Ken's ministry had his staff members play "Ken Shigs bingo." They laid out his twenty to twenty-five

---

5. Throughout this book we've attempted to introduce pastors by their full name in each chapter, with the references that follow by their first name. Different traditions place a greater or lesser emphasis upon titles (Reverend, Pastor, Doctor, etc.) and we have tried to strike a balance between properly introducing participants in the project without repetitive statement of titles.

6. His first book, *God in My Everything: How an Ancient Rhythm Helps Busy People Enjoy God*, is largely about how to pastor and live in a gentle and sustainable way.

favorite stories, and someone shouted "bingo" when they had them all: the shoplifting-as-a-kid story, the temptation-to-adultery story, and so on. Ken has shown us not to be afraid to repeat ourselves as preachers. Eventually the stories seep down in their bones. Perhaps only when they tease us for telling them too much have we told the key stories enough.

Some of those repeat stories are core to Tenth's identity. One is of a homeless man named Robert who was sleeping underneath the windows right outside Ken's office. A parishioner offered to let Robert live in his laneway house rent-free for the rest of his life (Jesus's people, doing Jesus things). Robert preferred the outdoors. One winter morning when office workers came to work, Robert was cold to the touch. He had frozen to death, right outside the church. Ken often tells of what he heard God the Holy Spirit say to him (and he usually tells it with his voice breaking slightly): if you bless those who cannot repay you, I will bless you. Tenth got busy learning from social-justice churches around the city how to serve its most vulnerable neighbors. Its regular meal ministry and its "Out from the Cold" offering of shelter on cold nights continue to this day. Ken is unwilling to let a painful lesson go to waste. That was Jesus sleeping outside the church. He will judge us all one day on how we treat him in his poor (Matt 25:31–46). Ken makes sure he uses his opportunity to speak for God in a way that doesn't let his people ever forget the lesson—even if his staff teases him a little for his repetitiveness. Ken tells us in an interview that he once got to ask the mayor of Vancouver, Philip Owen, what Tenth could do to serve the city better, expecting an answer around helping drug abusers rehabilitate. The mayor, a lifelong Anglican, suggested that Ken preach the gospel. The church serves the city by fostering an encounter with the love of God. What could be more urgent?

But Ken is no longer in a hurry. He saw a treacherous trajectory in his early frenzied efforts to resurrect the church on his own power. He's learned something of the patience of God, who let the people wander forty years, the exile stretched on for seventy, silence after the last prophet before the incarnation for three hundred. God is capable of a resurrection after three days, that's our signature story. But God can also wait to raise the rest of us for . . . God knows how long?!

Portsmouth Union Church in Portland is a sort of arranged marriage between what was once a dying United Methodist congregation with a building and a newer Evangelical Covenant congregation without one. These two congregations, one formerly more liberal, one formerly more conservative, have become one, with two part-time pastors. Historically, churches that amalgamate can become lowest-common-denominator places—seeking to please everyone, they thrill or challenge no one. Not so at Portsmouth Union. The Methodist half of the marriage has sought to give away its (precious!) property for housing for houseless neighbors. The one-time Covenant half, kicked out of that fellowship for its inclusivity, is now at a church with queer staff members and a woman pastor who insists she would never serve anywhere that wasn't affirming.

Yet Jules Nielsen and Andy Goebel have kept a sharp edge to their preaching. Christian faith makes you different from your neighbors, perhaps even a critical irritant in your neighborhood. Nielsen responds with fierce protectiveness when an outsider dunks on the church. She would have none of it. "Are you serious right now? Do you *know* how bad it is out there?" Any minister can outdo any outsider critic with stories of the church's failures (for real—ask us). But Jules grew up outside the church. "I didn't grow up with the option of mending, with a promise of hope, with a community alive and provisioned against despair, without redemption, without saving grace, where no one is coming to help you," she preaches. "I grew up in a people without forgiveness, with no span of time longer than your lifetime, where you got what you could, without a sense of God's time or the patience that comes from that." She sounds like a firebrand, doesn't she? "My faith community is bread to my soul, balm to my spirit, a light to my path. I've felt what captivity feels like, and any sacrifice I offer to the church tastes like freedom to me." This is, of course, no evangelical zeal floating above the realities of this painful age. PUC has been waiting for the city's permission to build that housing for years now. "The mayor calls housing an 'emergency,'" Nielsen marvels at the slowness. "This is stupid, we have to house them. It's stupid stupid stupid . . ." That urgency, that sense of hurry, comes from knowing houseless neighbors and longing for freedom with them. It also comes from having tasted life without God or God's people and remembering it as a sort of life without life.

Testimony must not be limited to clerical leaders, of course.[7] Ken Evers-Hood at Tualatin Presbyterian outside Portland asks his lay leaders to present their testimony as they step into leadership. Each has to write a statement of faith and to deliver it personally in front of the others. There is precedent for this, of course—membership in Puritan churches required testimony to the saving work of God within the believer at one time. But we mainline Christians are often tongue-tied precisely here (evangelicals can be better, though those "better" at testimony are often better copiers of the form). Evers-Hood finds that folks comply eventually and give articulate witness to their struggles in language that soars and leaves everyone in tears. This is crucial for working together as a leadership team, of course: "If I don't know what folks believe, how can we work together?"

Ken's preaching is a marvel. He preaches without notes, though that is not the thing (how often do people's comments about noteless preaching focus . . . on the notelessness? "Look ma—no hands!"). He heard Garrison Keillor once say that we preachers hide behind too much stuff. We have these bulky pieces of furniture and these elaborate robes and these essays we read from—all shields against . . . what? Memory loss? How important could it be if we forget to say it?! Ken has nothing against a good manuscript. He just doesn't use one. Preaching this way takes longer to prepare and requires real courage, but there is no going back.

His delivery comes off as natural, un-rehearsed even (you have to rehearse hard to achieve that!). One recent sermon took on the imposing Latin title, "Deus Absconditus," the hidden God. This is a key theme in the history of theology, but that way of putting it keeps the cookies on the high shelf. Ken spoke of the experience of God's absence. Of longing for God and hearing no answer. Testimony need not be happy. It can be full of sorrow, anger even. The psalmist rails against God for not answering. Mother Teresa heard nothing

---

7. See here Daniel, *Tell It Like It Is: Reclaiming the Practice of Testimony.*

from God after the voice on the train called her to care for the poorest of the poor—nothing *for years*. What if the church were honest about our experience of God being one of . . . darkness? "Though he slay me, yet I will praise him," Job insists (Job 13:15). I will preach nothing but Christ, and only him crucified, Paul declares (1 Cor 2:2). Testimony is not only of triumph. It is also, or even better, of sorrow—a "bright sadness," as Orthodox liturgy puts it.

Ken keeps two photos on the bookshelf opposite him, where he can see them from his desk. We assumed they would be family, kin, great friends. Instead, they are of church people he has lost. One is of Greg, a father of three, who took his own life. Another is of Zoe, a toddler who choked to death in an accident in the church's preschool. In one case, Ken preached of the glory of God that doesn't end with this life's end. In another he preached over a four-foot-long pink coffin. That was his hardest sermon. But where better to insist that the only good news is witness to the resurrection?

We two teach homiletics. And we have often taught that one source of holy urgency is awareness of our own coming deaths. If the preacher were to die on Monday, what will she have wished she said to them on Sunday? Preachers can hold back, leave something in reserve, as if trying to store up manna, forgetting that whatever is stored up will rot. One benefit of preaching this way is that one day it will come true. We will die. None of us gets out of this life alive. And none of us has as much time left as we wish we did. That's a risky homiletical principle—to preach in light of our fast-approaching death. Ken Evers-Hood sees our risky principle and raises us. Preach in light of *their* coming deaths. It will come for our hearers sooner than they, or we, would like. What should we say to them if this is the last word of hope they hear? No time for throat-clearing, corny jokes, theological side-quibbles, score-settling, time-killing, none of that. What is urgent? What is lifesaving and must be said *now*?

Father Matthew Tate gets at this holy urgency in a sermon on one of Jesus's miracles of raising the dead. Jesus is drawn toward suffering, Fr. Matthew points out. He seems not to be able to help himself. So, when a funeral procession blocks the disciples' way, his impulse is not what ours would be—how do we go around this snarl? He goes right into it (Luke 7:11–17). That's why he has come. This is why the Orthodox speak of Jesus as the "philanthropos," the lover of humanity.

Three times in the Lord's ministry he raised someone from death. We don't know what happened ontologically at that moment. Was a soul lifted up from Hades, deposited back in its body? The Orthodox have no Western notion of purgatory. The only way out of hell is to go with Jesus when he breaks down its gates, liberates the place, lifts out our foreparents, Adam and Eve. After Jesus's harrowing of hell, the gate of the joint is busted, no one is stuck inside. And a brief sign of this is Jesus's resuscitation of these three souls. Matthew says he believes every funeral is one in which Jesus places his hand on the funeral bier and offers resurrection life. It's just usually not so instantaneous for us as it is in the story. The three he raises will die again. And very few of us experience what they do. Based on Jesus's healing ministry, our chances are one in several billion that we'll be raised like this! But all of us can experience Jesus's usual way of life after death. Resurrection—it undoes our greatest urgency. Or what we thought our greatest urgency was.

Father Matthew describes himself as a convert from a slightly cultish, New Age-informed sect. He was working as a chaplain in a children's cancer ward in British Columbia. And he found that spiritual pablum insufficient to speak words of hope over a child's death. He discovered Orthodoxy from an interested Anglican priest, passing him books. And he plunged all the way in. The Orthodox Church bases its entire faith on the resurrection. That icon of Christ harrowing hell is the foundation of all the others. Death is inevitable. In Christ, life is more inevitable still.

If death is swallowed up by Christ, ministry looks different. It can be bold, free, non-anxious. Ron Clark, formerly of Agape Church of Christ in Portland, tells an example from a neighboring ministry in his city. Bridgetown Ministries started an initiative called Night Strike, in which church folks sought out those living under Portland's bridges. They would go and offer to wash feet. Odd as that sounds, it makes perfect sense theologically. The poor are Jesus Christ. Christians are called to serve him in them, them in him. That ministry (perhaps because of its oddity!) expanded to include the offering of haircuts, food, blankets, sleeping bags, clothing, prayers, conversation, and friendship. And not just church people are involved now. Life is contagious, desirable, when people spot it, they want it. The church's job is to offer it, to give it away.

Questions for Reflection and Action

1. How might the church act with urgency, and yet without hurry?
2. How does or might your congregation reclaim the practice of testimony? That is, of having non-pastors speak in public of their experience of the painful and tender mercy of God?
3. What should the church *run* after, like Philip or Abraham in the desert?

2

Evangelical and Liberal

A Necessary Paradox

It is a strange parochialism of our time and place in world and church history that "evangelical" and "liberal" are considered antonyms. To be an "evangelical" just means a conviction that the good news is really good news. Its hearing should make its hearers glad. God has come among us in Jesus Christ and blessed creation on the way to making all things new. "Liberal" just means "generous," expansive, lavishly prodigal, the way God is in Jesus's telling. Twentieth-century politics and culture wars in America pulled these terms apart, divided those which were never intended to be separate. But they belong to one another. The gospel's good news makes its recipients generous. There is no evangel without liberality; and perhaps, riskier now, no true generosity without the gospel.

American political operatives realized some fifty years ago that they could deploy religious terms as a cudgel to manipulate voters. Elections have been won, wars fought, the political tenor of a country and so the world changed that way.[1] But it's not terribly effective in Cascadia. There are social conservatives in eastern Washington and Oregon and in the interior of British Columbia. There are also social conservatives along I-5, Highway 99, and the coast. There

---

1. For a bit of the history have a look at Balmer, *Making of Evangelicalism*.

are even evangelicals in positions of public trust. But they are not enough, as a voting bloc, to swing elections. Washington and Oregon are safely Democratic states at election time. There may never have been Christendom in Cascadia.[2] Unlike most parts of North America, this region was not settled by Europeans coming for religious reasons. Playing the Jesus card will not get you elected here.

British Columbia has a premier from the New Democratic Party (NDP)—that is, from the party that receives support that Trudeau's liberals get elsewhere in the country. There is almost no Liberal Party in British Columbia. It's not liberal enough. But the NDP's founding father is one Tommy Douglas, premier of Saskatchewan, and more importantly for our purposes, a former Baptist pastor. He was doing youth work during the Great Depression and realized the street kids he was trying to reach needed decent health care more than entertainment. He got elected to the provincial legislature and got it passed. And the doctors went on strike. This was a socialist plot! (These scare tactics in the late twentieth century had earlier precedents, and not just in the USA.) But the people of Saskatchewan liked the health care. The doctors went back to work. Douglas got elected to national office and all of Canada's provinces adopted similar health plans (and, lest you worry overmuch, Americans, each province runs its own health care—it's not, technically, a national health-care system, but a province-by-province one). Douglas's flavour of early-twentieth-century social gospel faith was both evangelical and liberal. It was good news, which made its hearers more generous. Douglas was once voted the most beloved Canadian in history in a poll conducted by the Canadian Broadcasting Corporation.[3] More than Wayne Gretzky.

Ponder that for a minute.

Studying these missional churches in Cascadia, we were struck that they tied together these two impulses so often pulled apart in

2. So argues Lynne Marks in *Infidels and the Damn Churches*.

3. For real, check it: https://www.cbc.ca/archives/entry/and-the-greatest-canadian-of-all-time-is. Mssr Gretzky clocked in at #10. The list has some oddities: Don Cherry, the hockey broadcaster, found plenty of time since 2004 to discredit himself; and Alexander Graham Bell, at #8, didn't do most of his discovering *in* Canada . . .

wider North American culture. They are, at once, evangelical and liberal. They may be a harbinger for churches elsewhere. As Christendom disintegrates, and the dust lifts, churches that rise will hold these two impulses together: good news and generosity, evangelism and social justice.

Albert Chu's pulse seems to race as he describes the early days of planting Tapestry Church in Richmond, British Columbia. He and ten others had a vision for a multi-racial congregation but saw no existing congregation that quite lived up to that vision. So, they got busy "doing church. We were at our most missional ever at that point." They met in each other's living rooms, like the church in the New Testament. They joined local running clubs to make connections. They cooked for girls' soccer teams. Al sat in coffee shops for hours, using that vaunted office of church planters everywhere. Tapestry held public events celebrating the food and culture and clothes and trivia about different countries with immigrants in the neighborhood (Thailand first). They gave out balloons at a Canada Day event. They held barbeques. They would pass out "Tap water," bottled water with Tapestry's information on it (back before bottled water was passé). Al sounds like the writer of the book of Acts, nostalgic for a day that was. Tapestry has twelve hundred in worship now across four sites in greater Vancouver. Yet the blueprint of those early planting days is not gone. The building is just expanded now. Al is eager for Tapestry's latest church plant, in the Marpole neighborhood, to "start having babies." To find seventy or so folks presently driving too far to church and encourage them to do church, with others, in their neighborhood. "Planting is the engine of discipleship," Chu said.

Tapestry is not the only large church in Vancouver. Others are a good deal larger—Westside and Willingdon and Village churches look like American gigachurches. There are also first-generation immigrant churches that look a lot like congregations back home in Manila, Seoul, or Jakarta. What makes Tap remarkable is that it is a little of both. It is wholly Canadian, largely Asian, but genuinely multi-cultural. And unlike many gigachurches and immigrant churches, Tap has a bit of liberal to go with its evangelical. Chu himself went through a divorce in 2009. As a public and pastoral figure, this could have meant the end for a pastor in a certain kind of Christianity. Western Protestantism in effect replaced clerical celibacy with the expectation that a pastor have an idealized family. Conservative evangelicalism so frowns on divorce that going through one can poison a congregation or end a clerical career. Chu offered to resign. Tapestry instead gave him a year off to heal. He came back from plenty of therapy with a sense of grace that he offers freely to others. "It was good for the church," Al says now. "We want to be a safe place for broken people. And I didn't realize how depressed I was. We wouldn't have planted the last two or three times without that."

Tapestry has a practice of defaulting to "yes" in response to "weird asks." As a neighborhood, missional church, if its neighbors want to use its gathering space, or need a partnership on a community initiative, Tap is there. This is, mind you, over against the advice of some church-growth experts who suggest funneling the church's whole energy into a single area where it can make a difference. For example, a local upstart university asked Tap to design a multi-faith chaplaincy program. This could be a huge drain on time and resources. But with its default of yes, Tap accepted. Not just for evangelical purposes, but also to offer spiritual care to students of other faiths and of none. Some Tap members left in response to the multi-faith bit. "This was a way to give back, to meet international students. And it has helped us—interns from there have become staffers." But it hasn't helped Tap's worship numbers, despite offering Alpha and series like Jesus at the movies. It was a weird ask, a bold yes, and a partnership that only seems rare because of our strange times in North America: the gospel makes you generous. Liberal even.[4]

Not far from Tap is another multi-site and multi-racial evangelical congregation. Tenth Church's Ken Shigematsu might be Vancouver's most recognized pastor—not just among evangelicals, but among all of us. As we discovered in the last chapter, his twenty years of presiding over growth in a congregation that had been

---

4. There is a legacy of "liberal evangelical" language in the long history of the United Church of Canada, as Phyllis Airhart records in *A Church with the Soul of a Nation*, though it has fallen into disuse.

poised to close before his arrival is remarkable. He is a natural, nearly effortless, evangelist. It is hard to find a sermon that does not include an impassioned presentation of Jesus's saving work and invitation to follow in discipleship. But there is a difference from some other evangelical churches you may know. I defy you to find me a sermon in which Ken disparages any other faith. Tenth even changed its name from Tenth Avenue Alliance because a political party called itself Alliance, and Tenth goes out of its way to avoid the slightest whiff of partisanship. Ken's love for Jesus does not lead him to denigrate others, but rather to honor them. He is no culture warrior. In our interview he mentions a sermon he wrote against abortion. Not a surprise from an evangelical. This may be a surprise, however: he sent it to half a dozen pro-choice friends who work in the health care industry. He wanted to be sure he didn't mischaracterize anything and ran his text by those with opposing views.

Tenth has as one of its commitments a care for creation, which is often "evangelicalese" for distancing oneself from secular environmentalists. But Vancouver is the city that *birthed* Greenpeace. There is no gain to be had here from dunking on the environment. The unique thing here is Ken's evangelical addition to care for creation: he speaks of a beautiful painting gifted to him for an anniversary. It's by a respected local artist and worth some money, but worth far more to him for sentimental reasons. He treats it with absolute care and gentleness. He would never mistreat it. The inference is clear. God has blessed us with creation. It's not our possession. It possesses us, if anything. But if we treat our mere material possessions with such care, how should we treat this most precious gift?

Ken may be the master of the humblebrag. He is pleased that the religion reporter for the *Vancouver Sun*, Doug Todd, professes to be puzzled on where to classify him on the liberal/conservative grid. And he wants to find an elastic place between chaos and rigidity—a place of gospel freedom. We might see this most clearly in his efforts to stretch his congregation and denomination on inclusivity issues. Tenth, he says, was the first Christian and Missionary Alliance congregation in the world to have women elders. They were not yet allowed in the denomination, technically, but

Tenth elected them anyway and recorded and passed on their votes to national. Ken's succession plan at Tenth included the pronouns "he or she" before it was allowed for women to be senior pastors in the denomination. And there is a lively LGBTQ sub-community at Tenth. Ken has raised the question about whether queer members could participate in meaningful ministry as lay leaders. He figures the church accepts their money in the offering, why wouldn't the church accept their service?

This raises an obvious question: *why* would gay people bother to be at Tenth?! There are any number of affirming congregations and denominations in the city, some with rainbow flags over the front door (but an alarming lack of LGBTQ *people* inside). If someone far outside the church hears a church is now open to women or queers or whatever, they might just respond with a thumbs up and a shrug. Good for you, joining the twenty-first century. But they would never reconsider turning up or joining. Ken ponders and says this: "They feel the resonance of truth here. The welcome of community, the spiritual vitality. They discern the presence of God." On the other side of the spectrum, "if social justice is devoid of the beauty and power of Christ, it can still be a valuable thing, but not as unique as it is when the Holy Spirit illumines who Jesus is." Ken Shigematsu and Tenth Church are the perfect example of how to go forward on diversity. Don't do it by talking about diversity. Do it by talking about Jesus. And then see what sorts of diverse people Jesus draws to himself. And then get busy being the church together.

Perhaps the most remarkable example of the intertwining of evangelicalism and liberalism that we studied is Quest Church in Seattle. For years Jason pursued its founding pastor, Eugene Cho, for an interview about Quest's purchase of the former building owned by Mars Hill Church and its infamous misogynist pastor, Mark Driscoll.[5] Jason loved the idea of a story about comeuppance for a sexist pastor and media troll whose moral peccadilloes caught up with him. If you denigrate women from the pulpit, watch. A multi-ethnic church will take over your space and most of its

---

5. See, for example, Bruenig, "Failure of Macho Christianity."

pastors will be women, including one, Pastor Gail Song Bantum, who will preach in a Black Lives Matter T-shirt. The problem: Eugene wasn't interested. In fact, he had brushed off overtures from luminaries rather brighter than professors in Vancouver: journalists from *USA Today* and *Time* had made similar pitches. Quest wasn't interested in kicking dirt on anyone's grave. It was doing ministry in its neighborhood.

Cho left Quest not long ago and became head of Bread for the World, a major evangelical relief organization. You may have heard of his appearance on the national political scene as he denounced Donald Trump's description of COVID-19 as the "Chinese virus." The ethnic slur has led to disparagement and violence against Asian-Americans and should stop. The regular round of hate mail ensued.

Back at Quest, Pastor Gail has succeeded Eugene as senior leader of the church. This is not where she imagined she'd be. But looking back, it is perhaps the most natural thing that could have happened. Her Korean-American mother was a pastor before her, but was not affirmed in her call in conservative Korean immigrant churches. Gail's mother died when Gail was eighteen, which was "traumatic but redemptive": her being pastor of the largest Evangelical Covenant Church in America led by a woman feels like it has "redeemed her mother's prayers."

The Bantums arrived in Seattle for Gail's husband Brian to teach at a local university. They let their children choose their church. She was burnt out from pastoral work, seminary, and parenting and was glad to be anonymous for a while at Quest Church, but she couldn't escape. She recalled, "When Eugene and I started having conversations about joining the pastoral staff, I remember thinking to myself, 'I was not ready for a church led by a Korean man.'" She had come full circle. And now she leads the place. And she's not hiding her identity. "I'm an evangelical, Asian American, who deeply appreciates and engages womanist theology. I don't like when people try to name me or put me in a box. God's kingdom is so big, God can work through the unimaginable. We want folks to wonder, 'How can y'all be together?'"

When young Gail was reacting against her constraining church of origin, she found resonance and grace in Black Pentecostal churches. "There's a desperation in the worship. It feels like home. I was welcomed by a community not mine, so I have a heart for those who don't belong." She met Brian soon after she had lost her mother, and he had lost his father. Brian is bi-racial, working "in the between spaces, as a connector." Quest was perfect for them and their children to thrive. Pastor Gail was formed by the Black preachers who reintroduced the faith to her—not just with volume, but with playfulness, creative biblical exegesis, and passion. She is drawn to stories like "Ruth and Naomi: your people will be my people. The stories of non-belongers: of the Samaritan woman, the Canaanite woman." You can tell by looking at her staff: five out of six pastors are women, four are people of color—including Rev. Dr. Brenda Salter McNeil, a long-time luminary with InterVarsity Christian Fellowship, and Pastor Gail's right-hand preaching pastor.

There are, of course, other multi-ethnic churches in North America. They just tend to be led by white males, like most churches period. Quest shows how hard it is to be *genuinely* multi. When Pastor Gail first arrived at Quest the music ministry still was defaulting to the wider, white evangelical worship canon. Pastor Gail began to introduce gospel music and singing in other languages, to better reflect the diversity at Quest. Today, its worship style feels more African-American than anything, with a vaunted local music director from conservative Black churches. Yet those drawn to the gospel music faced a challenge: "You want us to sing in *Spanish*?!" Gail has praise for the white pastors on her staff with whom she shares high trust: they can name privilege without being reminded, can volunteer to take difficult meetings without being prodded. And Pastor Gail has made a priority what otherwise might have fallen off the table in stretching after so many multi's: LGBTQ+ inclusion. Quest is a member of the conservative Evangelical Covenant denomination. Yet when she was hired, Gail presented her vision for a church reaching far past that boundary. "I wanted to exercise authentic leadership and wouldn't have said yes if only 60 percent were ready. I wanted 85 percent." She needn't have worried. The vote went 87 percent in favor of hiring her. In terms of inclusion of queer people, the question at Quest "is not if, but how." They have long been there, of course (they're *everywhere!*).

Genuine difference is challenging. What college or business *doesn't* seek faces of different ethnicities for every glossy brochure? But actually making life together is another thing. Pastor Gail recounts the morning after the Charleston massacre, in which Black members were openly weeping before church even began. Others came to church unaware even that anything had happened, let alone an event as violent and triggering of genocidal memory as that. Before she was senior pastor, Gail preached on police brutality wearing that BLM T-shirt: "we had cops, and Black people who'd been stopped *that week,* in church." While the church loves her preaching style and content, there were enough comments on the T-shirt for her to be asked not to wear it again. Now she is more likely to wear the robe or stole of church officialdom. While male senior pastors may avuncularly disavow such symbols, people from historically excluded groups have less luxury to shrug them off. Gail's vision extends Quest's historic mission of challenging welcome, but not by activism alone: "Seattle doesn't turn its head at agitating!" There are unused offices at Quest that could become places for counseling, especially for burnt-out leaders of non-profits: "We want people to come to church for healing—to be *well*, not just to be members." Not a bad image for a time in the United States when fractures along lines of race and class are as painful as they are just now. "Justice without the gospel will create a binary. We're a Holy-Spirit formed, free and charismatic, liberation-centered, justice-minded" church. Gail pauses, and then shifts the metaphor: "We're a Pentecostal and justice fusion. We don't have to strategize for that, it's who we are." Perhaps Seattle will catch a whiff of that and want a taste.

Ron Clark, formerly of Agape Church of Christ in Portland, is no stranger to church growth. He helped lead a booming congregation in an affluent suburb. He speaks now of twenty years in that sort of ministry as a time when he was "focused on the wrong people."[6] Jesus's ministry is constantly with the marginalized, upsetting people in power. So, Ron left his previous work to start Agape,

6. See his work *The God of Second Chances: Finding Hope through the Prophets of Exile.*

which from the outset would be a "Luke 4" church. That is, it would take part in Jesus's announcement of Isaiah's vision: release to the captives, recovery of sight to the blind, the oppressed going free, all part of the year of the Lord's favor (4:18). He told his denominational superiors in the Church of Christ that Agape would grow big. While supporting him, they also let him down easy: "No you won't." Agape never did. The Sunday we visited had maybe two dozen people, counting generously. Not long after that visit, Ron stepped away from its leadership to train church planters for the denomination. But he has -nly words of comfort for the small congregation. They are often made to feel guilty, like they are doing it wrong. Countless church growth seminars suggest this or that tweak to unlock fantastic growth, like some kind of ponzi scheme. Missional will not necessarily mean big. In fact, social-justice churches will likely stay small, and may even close, as Agape may, post-Ron (a few dozen folks are trying to keep the flag flying). But Ron points out that schools are also struggling to get parents onto PTA. Athletic coaches are struggling to find players. Getting involved in communities is down across the board. Ron Clark's ministry is one that undercuts guilt. How else can you work with people who have been told they're worthless?

The Church of Christ is quite a conservative denomination. It is part of the restorationist movement, which so worried about country-club Christianity that it not only outlawed pipe organs—a nineteenth-century symbol of affluence embraced by other churches. It outlawed accompanying music altogether. Clark speaks of the expense and energy needed to gather a worship band as a reason Agape did not have one, yet one is charmed at its openness about its roots. Only a capella singing in here. If that's charming, what comes next will make you ugly cry. A woman stands and tells the congregation she has little time to live. She once prostituted herself for a living, though now she intends to spend what time she has left rebuilding broken relationships. While she faces the end of her cancer, she means to make amends with those she has hurt, including an estranged daughter. The entire congregation gathers and lays hands on her to pray. Others have laid hands on her for money. She stands proud now, with no guilt, thanking God for his goodness to her. Some might scoff—a former prostitute with no time to live? Of course, she "found Jesus." Yet here she is in the place of honor. Ron says the church had some half a dozen folks in prostitution involved in the church at one time. Here some of the people dearest to Jesus's heart find welcome in an actual church. The vision of Luke 4 lives.

Ron's work is not only one of joining evangelicalism and liberalism, the gospel and inclusion. It also raises the stakes by including academic theology. He has a doctorate in Bible, regularly presents papers to the Society of Biblical Literature, and writes books on the Scriptures, usually using his own translations from Hebrew and Greek. His unique vantage helps him to see as few others can. St. Paul speaks of his regular beatings and other hardships: "He's a trauma survivor. He would have had nightmares, PTSD, he'd have been emotionally fragile. I teach chaplains that. There's a reason he's preoccupied with resurrection." He speaks of an online Bible study with those trying to leave the sex industry (there was a reason for Zoom before COVID-19 even!). Teaching about Rahab and mentioning the scholarly consensus that most Genesis stories are not straight history, his hearers disagree. "I don't know about the scholarship, but this isn't an invented character. She does everything like a prostitute. She manipulates well." Seeing Exodus through abuse-survivors' eyes, Jesus's ministry with houseless persons, the minor prophets with sufferers from intimate partner violence, the list goes on. Ron's biblical exegesis crackles with life because of the people with whom he reads the bible.

You won't be surprised to learn that Agape has been involved in international short-term mission projects. University Presbyterian in Seattle may have invented the two-week jaunt to Central America to paint houses. "Missionary" had once meant a lifelong calling; in the last generation it means an alternate spring break trip. Ron has traveled to Malawi to teach, where he presented some of what he had learned about intimate partner violence, from a biblical vantage. His hosts and friends in Malawi were reluctant to hear him on such "issues," saying "We're more focused on evangelism." Notice the bifurcation between evangelical and liberal has been spread far beyond its North American origin. This wasn't the first time Ron had heard this objection. He had verses ready to go from

Proverbs about God ignoring the prayer of the violent man: "You won't make it to heaven if you're abusing your wives." They paused. One bravely spoke up and said, "We need to speak out about this!" Another one-time unpromising audience was from Russia. One of Ron's books on intimate-partner violence had been translated into Russian, but Russian pastors said this problem was not a Russian one—perhaps the Westerners would like the books back? But there are some 100,000 members of the Russian diaspora just in Portland. A women's group working on domestic violence found Ron, had him interviewed and put in a magazine, and then a *local* groundswell for his book emerged. The Russian copies already existed, and now had a purpose. Local police wanted to use the book, since local "advocates say there is no faith-based domestic violence material for Russian speakers." But there is now—an intense love for the Bible and desire to protect the vulnerable belong together. Marry them, and watch who will be blessed, not just around the world, but right under your nose.

Oh, and Ron understands criticism of conservative churches. He has plenty—it's why he turned to a grittier, social justice-model of church. Yet he adds this proviso: "The people building homeless villages are conservative. We had one Unitarian show up one time. That was great! But not a lot of folks who are big into social justice show up. If a church has a conservative view of the Bible, I can make clear to them that this is an issue."

Perhaps missional churches after Christendom can show that evangelism and liberalism were never divided. They only seemed to be. When I tell Jules Nielsen that her preaching sounds more "evangelical" than I'd expected from an LGBTQ+-inclusive Methodist pastor, she laughed. "Everywhere I go, progressives think I'm evangelical and evangelicals think I'm too liberal. My answer is, 'Well, I guess if you meet Jesus, you're probably both. And neither." In one recent sermon, Jules mused about Jesus's command to become like a little child. Stained-glass makers who depict children as well-kept blond cherubs may never have met an *actual* child. But Jules has. One kid in her former church was, she admits, her "favorite. I know I'm not supposed to say that." And one Sunday-school session left her favorite in tears. Not the spiritual kind. Broken down.

Non-functioning. She gets that way sometimes (who doesn't?). Jules found her in a corner in the fetal position, not moving. So even though it was time to get to the sanctuary and into a robe to *do her job*, Jules lay down on the floor with the child, trying not to think about how she was late to the service she planned. *This* was her job just then—being down on the floor with the vulnerable. Finally, the girl let the pastor hold her, "and that's when I learned that children can be Rhesus monkeys." The child wouldn't let go. She had quit sobbing but was still sniffling. But Jules had to preside and preach. So, she did. With a Rhesus monkey on her hip all morning. Folks told her they might not remember the content, but they would never forget the image of a preacher with a child on her hip, snot on her shirt, talking about a God of welcome. Jesus never said we had to be a well-behaved, composed, with-it child. Just a child. Clinging to her mama with every limb. Irrationally (or is this perfectly rational?) unwilling to let go.

Questions for Reflection and Action

1. What are commitments your church holds together that might seem like contradictions, or "liberal" and "evangelical" polar opposites?
2. Discuss work your church has done with the vulnerable that has changed how you read the Bible, and vice-versa?
3. Is there a "weird ask" to which your congregation might say "yes," and so birth new life and relationships?

3

All the Sacred Cows (and Great Preachers) Are Dead

We both moved here from what Cascadians call "back east." Whether it was Ontario or North Carolina, the experience can be a similar one, as Christian leaders try to figure out what it means to minister on the West Coast. At times, it felt like having a trap door open and falling from a position of community respect to one of as much value as the guy in the old 1980s Maytag repairman commercials. Back east, we were regularly invited to civic functions, consulted by the small-town mayor, or asked to speak to the local Chamber of Commerce on matters of community significance. In Cascadia, the thought of asking a Christian leader to open meetings with prayer or seek their counsel is never even considered. However, asking an indigenous elder to pray before a gathering is now mandatory.[1] Back east, ministry was seen more as a noble profession, complete with our clergy parking spot and shiny ID badge

1. Our colleague at The Vancouver School of Theology Professor Ray Aldred (Director of the Indigenous Studies Program) delights in reminding people that a majority of indigenous people in Canada identify as Christian *and* indigenous. So, in a "secular society" asking an indigenous elder to pray may just be inviting Jesus into a public space.

(just like a real doctor!) at the local hospital. In Cascadia, we soon learned that local clergy were thought of as odd if we asked for any recognition or status from the hospitals, something like a problematic family member coming too often to visit. Indeed, over a decade ago a local health official in the Vancouver area, Fraser Health CEO Nigel Murray, eliminated all paid chaplains (or the more updated title of "spiritual care worker") from the hospitals, citing their work as providing no value and telling those who protested "not to waste their breath."[2]

Back east, our ministries could still benefit from the fumes of Christendom swirling in the air, with non-churchgoing "cultural Christians" still accessing the church for rites of passage ranging from baptisms to weddings to funerals. It was not uncommon for the church office telephone to ring and for someone to say, "Hi Reverend, we're just in town today with our new baby visiting my Grandma who goes to your church. Can we swing by the church later and have the kid done?" Always tempted to reply, "medium or well-done?" these requests for baptism simply did not materialize after moving to the West Coast. The telephone did not ring. Weddings too were few and far between. Where it was most obvious was with funerals. Back east, the working relationship between clergy and funeral directors was often a close and personal one. Seen with a similar community leadership role, working odd hours for the care of families and offering pastoral support for those in deep grief, united many of us clergy with our funeral-director colleagues. Besides, the boozy Christmas parties and annual funeral director's golf tournament were a great hangover of Christendom. In Cascadia, however, it became clear immediately that the relationship, if any, was purely transactional. In fact, often funeral directors would "cut out the middleman," pocketing the officiant's fee and offering instead to "say a few words" as Master of Ceremonies at the "celebration of life." Now, this may sound like clergy griping, but in fact funeral directors in Cascadia are simply reflecting the more secular nature of the culture. Back east, if Grandma died and you hadn't been to church in years, the funeral director's suggestion of calling

2. Todd, "Health Authority Ignores Research," para. 12.

a trusted minister of the funeral home (no hellfire and brimstone preaching please) was often met with grateful approval. But here in Cascadia, if you've never been to church in your life (and your deceased Grandma probably didn't attend either) why would you ever consider having a Christian officiant? You might as well order up a singing telegram or a clown who does children's birthday parties. No, in fact, if you scan the obituaries in our Pacific Northwest newspapers, you'll find that, on average, one-third of deaths have no public gathering of remembrance with the common phrase, "no service by request"; one-third will have some sort of "celebration of life" with a glass of wine at the country club; and one-third will have some sort of spiritual event in a place of worship or the infamous funeral-home chapel with its intentionally opaque look of being "like a church" but not specific to any faith tradition.

All that to say, an important aspect to acknowledge about Christian witness in Cascadia is that the cultural landscape is quite unlike (or perhaps simply further ahead of) the rest of North America in its secularization. This movement, however, has been a cause of concern not only here in the Pacific Northwest for Christian leaders, but has been well studied and written about for years in Canada and the United States using the biblical metaphor of exile. Old Testament scholar Walter Bruggemann has long been associated with this move to describe the relocation of the Christian church from the center of society, with its access to political and cultural power, to the margins in the late twentieth and early twenty-first centuries. In making connections to the biblical theme of exile, Bruggemann and others have identified not only this loss of prestige and purpose in the wider society, but the crisis it evoked in Israel (and in the church today) regarding core understandings of faith. King Nebuchadnezzar's first invasion of Israel in 597 BC and subsequent invasion and destruction of Jerusalem (including the temple) in 586 BC created conditions of not only temporal and material jeopardy but also existential angst in the population, both those left behind in the smoldering ruins of David's city and the best and brightest hauled off to Babylon. As Stefan Paas notes,

> To Israel this was not just a cultural and political trauma; it was also an attack on the foundations of their faith. With the destruction of the temple and the termination of the sacrifices God disappeared from their midst; with the collapse of David's dynasty God's promise that there would always be a son of David on the throne was rendered undone; and with the occupation of the land God's promise to the patriarchs fell apart. In the words of Walter Brueggemann, this was for ancient Israel "the end of privilege, the end of certitude, the end of domination, the end of viable political institutions, and the end of a sustaining social fabric . . . it was the end of life with God, which Israel had taken for granted."[3]

This narrative of exile and decline has impacted Christianity across the denominational spectrum. In the (formerly) mainline churches, the narrative has resonated deeply. Many within the Reformed and Episcopal traditions have used this as the dominant lens to interpret their own uprooting and displacement from society when they reflect back on the high-water mark of membership, attendance, financial strength, and cultural influence of the 1950s and 1960s. For many within the mainline traditions of middle- and upper-class status still involved in church today, the description of having the "best and the brightest" hauled off to Babylon like Daniel or Meshach, Shadrach, and Abednego fits like a glove. The best days are behind us and we are muddling through.

Dean Emeritus of St. Andrew's Hall Stephen Farris is fond of telling a story of preaching in a "tall steeple" Canadian church, once full to overflowing in the sixties and now almost empty on a Sunday. Shaking hands after church, an older gentleman firmly took Stephen's hand and seized his forearm, shaking them enthusiastically. Stephen, a renowned professor of homiletics and powerful preacher, was expecting the usual "thank you for the sermon, Reverend" but instead the man offered this response. Nodding his head firmly and with steely determination in his eyes the man said, "All the great preachers . . . are dead!" Well, there probably is some truth to that, if by great preachers we imagine "pulpit princes/princesses"

---

3. Paas, *Priest and Pilgrims*, 125–26.

in dark robes preaching to masses (with their hats and white gloves on). Yes, all the great preachers are dead, and so too are the sacred cows of Christendom—cultural legitimacy, political influence, financial health, pews that repopulate themselves with each successive generation, and a perceived need by the wider society of our value and necessity as church.

Of course, not everyone in the church in North America has so readily bought into the exile motif. If mainline Protestants have taken the copyright out on exiles in Babylon (along with a monopoly on Micah 6:8), anabaptists who have always been wary of courting political and cultural power might best be described as those "left behind" in Jerusalem. The cultural landscape is not any more kind or beneficial to those who were less advantaged by the Christendom power-sharing model of state and church, however anabaptists have learned ways of forming thicker community without relying on cultural conditioning. This is also true for Roman Catholics outside of Quebec in Canada, and especially here on the West Coast.

For exiles in Babylon, Scripture acknowledges that there were different ways of interpreting relocation. This is also true for our context. For example, there have been successive waves of reaction against the secularizing influence upon the church in society, primarily by evangelical Christian communities. Just as Hananiah promised a speedy return to Jerusalem and restoration of the good life, so too the church-growth movement and megachurch thinking saturated the market in the 1980s and 1990s with every conference book table and keynote offering tips and tricks on how to attract people to your hip and relevant Christian church. Vancouver missiologist Alan Roxburgh has long warned about these never-ending attempts to turn back the ecclesiastical clock or plug a hole in the leaking levee with a Michael W. Smith CD from the 1980s. Roxburgh warned in publications as early as *Missional: Joining God in the Neighborhood* about the tendency of churches to meet this new cultural reality of exile by applying technical rationality, adopting management and control techniques borrowed from the business world, asking the wrong "churchy" questions with an ecclesiocentric focus and seeing the world too narrowly through clergy-centric leadership. In more recent work, such as *Practices for the Refounding of God's People*, Roxburgh takes equal aim at the mainline and evangelical churches with a critique of the preferential biblical metaphor of exile itself, noting that the North American churches have not been uprooted and taken to a hostile land, but rather they have stayed put and failed to adapt to the culture around them over the last several decades. He suggests adopting the biblical model of sojourner, as evidenced in Abraham and Sarah's story, journeying through a new cultural space as guest might better apply. Churches are now trying to make sense of speaking faith in a Western context where a normal, healthy, full, and meaningful life with God is possible (and often easier to embrace), focused instead on "faith" in the state, consumer capitalism, and the self. The encouraging news is that in the course of our research we discovered ample evidence of Christian communities tacking in the direction of a life lived with and for the Triune God, that was deeply rooted within this cultural context, without being set against it.

Beyond dry ice and lasers, purity rings and WWJD bracelets, there are so many within the evangelical world today who acknowledge that the return from exile will not be quick, easy or painless. In fact, we discovered so many mainliners, anabaptists, and evangelicals in our research who were keen to turn away from Hananiah's "ten easy steps to a successful ministry" and instead pushed their chips to the center on Jeremiah's advice to hunker down in this new cultural reality. By finding new ways to worship, work, and witness, it is possible to experience the grace and goodness of God following Jeremiah's prophetic revelation from the Lord to

> build houses and settle down; plant gardens and eat what they produce. Marry and have sons and daughters; find wives for your sons and give your daughters in marriage, so that they too may have sons and daughters. Increase in number there; do not decrease. Also, seek the peace and prosperity of the city to which I have carried you into exile. Pray to the Lord for it, because if it prospers, you too will prosper.[4]

4. Jer 29:5–7, NIV.

Far from throwing up their hands in hopelessness or doubling down on attractional model techniques from Willow Creek, the Christian communities we studied acknowledged the strange new world of Cascadia while embracing the opportunity to follow Jesus in a new way.

Sitting in the former Mars Hill building in Seattle where Mark Driscoll once offered a toxic form of megachurch revival, Senior Pastor Gail Song Bantum at Quest Church remarks that there was no cultural Christianity left in the city when she arrived. Instead, ministry requires starting from ground zero. Christians should expect not only hostility towards the claims of the gospel but cynicism too. Even in the so-called "none" zone, Song observes that you still find enough de-churched people arriving from other parts of North America who long ago gave up on the institutional church. Song tells us how much she loves hearing how "people who once were jaded or hurt or excluded by previous churches and their leaders find home and haven at Quest, and they see a glimmer of hope in God and God's people again. Nothing brings me greater joy as a pastor." In other words, the goals of an attractional church with its consumer-orientated mindset of friendly baristas serving good coffee, contemporary music, "relevant" preaching, and church buildings, language, and programs that stripped down the tradition to make it more palpable to a Sunday School dropout, no longer works (if it ever really did at all). Instead, leading a church of over seven hundred with the average age of participant in their mid-thirties, Song notes, "We are not a perfect church, but we want to be a desperate church—desperate for the miraculous, the 'more than we could imagine' kind of manifestations of God's power and presence in the world; we seek to embody the fullness of what we believe the kingdom of God looks like and lives out in tangible ways." Song is clear that a commitment to mission is key for congregations moving away from an attractional model of church. She reflects on what has made Quest different in its expression of mission and ministry in that community:

> Our mission is to love people wholeheartedly, love God boldly, and make disciples faithfully. We want people to

feel and experience a sense of belonging, so we press for radical love of neighbor. From that space of belonging, we believe that people will have a greater capacity to trust and believe in a God who is seen and felt by the people who love them, that we might then become the fullness of all that God has created and gifted us to be in the world as followers of Christ.

Song acknowledges that for many churches the shift to missional incarnational engagement can feel intimidating or even overwhelming, but she encourages congregations to start somewhere and to start local. She says, "Being actively engaged in the things that are happening in our cities, country, and the larger world around us is crucial. We can't do everything, but we can all engage in something. . . the church should bear witness to the healing and restorative work of God's kingdom in the here and now."

Across the city in the South Lake Union neighborhood of Seattle, Union Church pastors James B. and Renee Notkin describe their context as ministering in the carcass of Christendom. There is much to be salvaged and repurposed from the legacy we've inherited but there is also much more to be left behind and let wither away. For the Notkins, planting a PC-USA congregation in downtown Seattle out of University Presbyterian Church, the struggle has often been around deciding what to hold onto and how to critically and theologically think about that legacy of Christendom. At Union Church, they have responded by creating a mixed-use space in their warehouse building, purchased a few years before Amazon decided to make the neighborhood their world headquarters. They describe South Lake Union today as "an urban high-tech neighborhood in downtown Seattle. It is a neighborhood that is in constant change and confused about its identity. There are people in our community who live on the margins and receive social services as well as some of the most expensive housing in the area." In the first third of the building is Kakao—a coffee shop with a specialty of good quality chocolate. In the back two-thirds of the building, known as 415 Westlake, is a venue with a full kitchen for music, receptions, corporate and cultural events. This is also where Union Church worships on Sunday mornings.

Throughout the old warehouse are high ceilings, sturdy brick walls and a sense of heritage that many old churches value, but those other traditional ecclesiastical spaces too often serve instead as barriers to those who are not Christian. Here, the wider community comes in on a daily basis. Renee reflects on how the space has created the community saying,

> We are a motley crew. We are messy. We are a bunch of broken people discovering that the grace of Jesus is all we have. We also are a beautiful sign of the body of Christ with people willingly sharing of their beautiful gifts, personalities, backgrounds, passions. Whenever our Union community (in whatever fashion or number of folks) is gathered I am overwhelmed by how together we reveal the goodness, healing hope and restoration of the Kingdom of God in ways that cannot be experienced alone. I also find that our space as a cafe and venue during the week provides an oasis and also foretaste of who God desires us to be.

Sitting and talking with James B. and Renee, it is clear that the prestige and power of Christendom has been set aside long ago, replaced instead with an expectation that God will show up and lead. You hear their awe at the work of God in their midst and the acknowledgment of the limits of human agency when they say things like, "The Holy Spirit shows up everywhere—in conversations, in provision of resources, in surprise encounters, in forgiveness, in willingness to be vulnerable, in hearts that are broken by racism, violence, division and suffering in our world, in children who dance with abandon to our worship band . . . the Holy Spirit shows up everywhere."

Ken Evers-Hood in Portland seems to operate out of a similar curiosity about what God was doing beyond the church in the community and sought to meet God in those places. He too resonates with the language of the "carcass of Christendom." He's deeply rooted and invested in the mainline church tradition but is not looking for it to continue and keep him comfortable. He has a holy restlessness and is surprised when he visits churches that appear to be content with the status quo. "Churches like that are just floating, and that's dangerous," he says. "I keep telling them they're a year older every year, they die a little when they're not growing." Instead he offers the advice to pay attention to what brings you alive as a person and a congregation. He insists that church leaders must be responsible for their own spiritual formation and networking. He's tired of denominational gatherings where people meet, pray, and whine about parishioners. Instead he asks, "What are you doing to feed the congregation? What are you passionate about and how can you use what brings you alive to bless the congregation? Where is God at work around you that together you can point and say, 'Look, there's evidence of God'?" For example, Ken designs gatherings known as storytelling nights in locations outside of the church building like a coffeeshop or bar, where spoken word poets and storytellers come with porous boundaries to connect. Ken notes that his church follows three watchwords (really four, he teases): generous community, adventuring, and buoyancy. He reflects on starting the first food pantry in Tualatin and how it led the way on establishing Family Promise, helping re-house families experiencing homelessness. Ken says, "By adventuring we mean we are a community where questions are welcome, and we acknowledge everyone is at a different place along the way. And buoyancy refers to our desire to be a community that brings people together and lifts them up with joy, hope, and laughter."

Like Gail Song Bantum at Quest Church in Seattle, Ken has also consistently made room for those who are exploring faith from a place of hurt or disillusionment. He says, "We are a place where people who have been hurt by other expressions of the church or who just assumed Christians were narrow asshats can come, actually feel grace, be who they are, and they can begin to have a relationship with Jesus (or not) in a loving, welcoming environment." As a PC-USA pastor, he notes that the welcoming environment doesn't mean that anything goes theologically. Instead he is quick to add, "I'm fairly orthodox personally, so this isn't like Jesus-light. The feeling is more of if Judas was welcome at the table then who am I to say someone shouldn't be showing up? We also have translated this hospitality into our hands-on work in the community."

Back in Seattle, we sit with James B. and Renee talking about their ministry in the neighborhood, while the coffee shop buzzes with life and caterers setting out wine glasses for a music concert in the back space that evening. We note how interesting it was that there were no signs or reference anywhere to the fact that a Presbyterian Church both owned the building and worshiped there on Sunday. It felt less "Christian coffeeshop," with lattes being served with the sign of the cross in frothy milk and Chris Tomlin songs playing in the background, and more reflective of the young, highly diverse, lanyard-wearing tech and Amazon employees who work and live in the neighborhood. The Notkins insist that their aim is to seek the welfare and common good of the neighborhood from corporate executives, musicians seeking a place to perform or those who come to access the space weekly as a women's shelter. Renee pondered, "How does a six-year-old view God differently because they know that the place where they sing songs on Sunday is also the place where women sleep on Monday evening? In a time when there is increased polarity 415 Westlake is a redeemed space given by God as a place of radical hospitality." The ministry couple explain how they've developed a worshiping, witnessing, working community of disciples in a so-called secular neighborhood over the years by integrating discipleship practice and community witness. They talk about the changing rhythm of their Sunday gatherings.

On the church's app the pattern is described this way: "Worship is our life lived in response to God's love for us and God's passion for justice and reconciliation. We live in a rhythm that reflects that. Worship expands our imagination to more fully take in the reality of God. That not only happens with music, prayer, and Scripture, but also through loving and serving others in partnership with the Holy Spirit. That's why every Sunday at Union is a little different. We're in a rhythm that reinforces a broad experience of worship." The app goes on to explain what one can expect when joining them on any given particular Sunday with the first, third, and fifth Sundays as a time of worship through music, prayers, story, and Scripture with the goal of having their lives re-orientated by Jesus and his message. The Lord's Supper and prayer circles are also included on these three Sundays. The second Sunday of the month is focused on connecting with one another in community. There is music, prayer, and a brief message, but the majority of the time is spent in small groups discussing the theme of the day and God's activity in their lives.

The fourth Sunday is described as worshiping "together through action." Renee says of this Sabbath gathering that it "continually stretches us and invites our community to risk as we take one Sunday a month to come alongside others in our community. As we go out into the community to lead hymn-sings in retirement homes, provide brunch at Seattle Cancer Care Alliance, make lunches for a homeless day center and rake our neighbors leaves, we learn that we worship God in the context of our community and not in isolation." James B. notes that this fourth Sunday has likely had the greatest evangelistic impact on the church over the years. If there is a Sunday that people feel most comfortable inviting a friend along, it's the fourth Sunday. Often from this experience of serving others alongside Christians, people begin to ask questions and find their way into the other Sundays and eventually baptism into the body of Christ. It's also an important way the church learns more about their neighbors. Renee says that for them it has been important to genuinely get to know the neighborhood without strings attached. That every church should find a way to do that. Genuinely listening to your congregation and community and holding their stories as precious and real. According to Renee, this involves "Inviting people on a journey toward wholeness that takes us outside the walls of the church onto the streets and dwellings of our communities where Jesus has already gone before us. Embracing our differences with joy and openness to learn and grow." In many ways, James B. and Renee's worship rhythm acknowledges that faith comes from hearing, saying, and doing. This echoes missional thinkers like Darrell Guder who notes the importance of Jesus's imperative, "be my witnesses" as a mission statement of what the church is to be, do and say.[5]

Back in Portland, Ken Evers-Hood shows us a book he had his Session read together entitled *Unlikely: Setting Aside Our*

5. Guder, *Be My Witnesses*, 44.

Differences to Live Out the Gospel. It tells the story of how Portland's (openly gay) Mayor Sam Adams proactively sought out a friendship with Kevin Palau (son of famous evangelist Luis Palau). Adams, who wrote the foreword to the book, and Palau built a partnership between evangelical churches, political leaders, school officials, the LGBTQI community, and others for the welfare of the city. In a city as secular as Portland, the book profiles the incredible transformation that took place in examples like Roosevelt High School where a local school was partnered with an evangelical church. Through volunteers, coaching, mentorships and sweat equity the two communities invested in each other and blessed the neighborhood, turning around a school that was failing and developing lifelong friendships in the process between students and church members. Putting aside the usual "hot button issues" that too often break down these community partnerships, Ken noted that the Christians involved in the project were guided by Jesus's life of radical inclusiveness that would have been well beyond the socially and religiously acceptable activities for a rabbi of his day.

Even in Cascadia there is evidence of Christians crossing the so-called "secular divide" to build partnerships with others of different or no faith background. This kind of public work can scramble all kinds of assumptions we have about Christian witness in the Pacific Northwest. Take even something as common in Christendom culture such as "prayer breakfasts" in the United States. These events started as efforts to gather politicians and business leaders in order to be an influence for Christ. But they have often been hijacked by a political agenda, usually narrowly partisan (for example, when Donald Trump showed up and said Donald Trump sorts of things at the event in Washington in 2019). It may surprise you to know we have a prayer breakfast in British Columbia. And politicians show up. And say nice things about religion. Sometimes the Lieutenant Governor of British Columbia shows up, representing the Queen herself. There's a big-deal speaker, everyone plays dress up, the food isn't bad for a thousand-person event, and church leaders go away feeling like what we do is important.

The thing is, these events represent the epitome of religious capitulation to modernity. By design, nothing political is said (we don't have Trumpism in British Columbia thankfully. Not yet anyway). Political leaders from multiple parties stand and say how nice it is not to have reporters in the room. They wax sympathetic about each other's long hours and the strain on family that comes with public service. They trot out dusty jokes about church that they don't often get to use ("this year we've had floods and hurricanes. No locusts or frogs yet").

None of this is bad. Public servants do work long hours to bless their neighbors. They do deserve thanks and respect from the rest of us. Speakers doing excellent ministry deserve attention and fundraising opportunities. Breakfast deserves to get eaten, ties and pantyhose to get worn, Lieutenant Governors to be stood for (and, please, pronounce the "f" in lieutenant). Pastors deserve a little recognition. There are undersides (what politician doesn't want to be in front of one thousand civic leaders at 8 am?!). But no more so than any other sort of chamber of commerce event.

But none of this requires the resurrection of Jesus to *work*.

Christendom assumed these events were ipso facto good. We stroke our leaders' egos and in return we get some cultural or even legal influence. No more. They turn up for their time at the microphone, they stroke us back, but they would not be caught dead letting us in on their authority. Note how different this is than Kevin Palau's partnership with the mayor of Portland. Similar initiatives between churches and governments have brought about care for the poor in Seattle and Vancouver. These efforts can result in genuine and hard-won partnership that blesses the city's neediest neighbors, who, when the chips are down, tend not to be helped by atheists over much. The end of Christendom and its self-congratulatory parades of meaningless prayers and jokes and finery can make for genuine missional partnerships. This is not wishful thinking. In this book we have names and addresses to prove it.

Christians engaged in the community, transforming lives and looking for areas described by Canadian philosopher Charles Taylor as "overlapping consensus," has provided Cascadian Christians will all kinds of opportunities in the public arena that would not have otherwise been seen to be possible. The difference, however, is that unlike in Christendom, these opportunities are not assumed, and power is not automatically granted. These opportunities come through investing locally in relationships in matters that are important for the common good. In Vancouver, for example, the Roman Catholic Archbishop Michael Miller formed a friendship with Mayor Gregor Robertson in 2015 over their shared values regarding care for creation. The timing was right in light of Pope Francis's encyclical *Laudato Si*, which offered a withering critique of global capitalist greed and big industry's mistreatment of the environment and the poor. Mayor Robertson, famous for biking everywhere, joined with hundreds of indigenous leaders, environmentalists, charities, and faith leaders for a symposium at the John Paul II Pastoral Centre. "The impacts of climate change are already taking place and are devastating," noted Robertson. The archbishop concurred, saying, "We have a common desire and intention to address the harm we have inflicted on the Earth. We have abused the gifts of God."[6]

Back in Seattle, Gail Song Bantum and Quest Church are building partnerships with those detained for illegal immigration and being held at a notorious Immigration and Customs Enforcement (ICE) detainment facility south of the city in Tacoma. Many have rallied to their social-justice initiative, having ears to hear how Christians are in solidarity with those who are mistreated and suffer because they serve a Savior with the taste of death in his mouth and wounds in his hands and feet. For all of the pastors we spoke to who were finding traction within the wider public arena, there wasn't a trace of Christendom delight in being around "the powerful and influential." In fact, quite the opposite. Ken Shigematsu laughed and said he didn't feel trapped doing what he was doing at all, teasing he could always go back to working as an executive at Sony. So too with Gail Song Bantum at Quest Church who quipped, "Some days I think I'd rather go work at Facebook and make some money." These Cascadian pastors who are making a real impact on their community tend to wear the mantle lightly, knowing that in post-Christendom North America relying on human agency has obvious limits. Instead, in a cultural context where all the sacred

6. Todd, "Climate Is Changing," paras. 9, 6.

cows (and great preachers) are dead, they are free to live and serve relying instead on the active, saving, redeeming action of Father, Son and Holy Spirit in the world.

Questions for Reflection and Action

1. Can you name the sacred cows still "alive" in your congregation, and what might you have to do to leave them behind?
2. What is something risky your community of faith has done recently for the sake of the gospel?
3. What is the dominant biblical story (lens) that your congregation sees itself and the world through these days?

4

Missional Leadership of Heart and Mind

A former student was eagerly anticipating his ordination in the first week of Lent. He shared a story of coming out of an Ash Wednesday service and walking home along the busy streets of downtown Vancouver. A man on the sidewalk stopped beside him as they waited for the light to change in order to cross the street. "Hey," the stranger said, "why do I see so many people with all that weird black stuff all over your forehead?" The soon-to-be-ordained minister told him it was Ash Wednesday, and that Christians were marking the beginning of the season of Lent leading to Easter and a celebration of Jesus's resurrection. The man wasn't impressed with the answer. He frowned. The traffic light changed and as the ash-covered Christian crossed the street the inquisitive man yelled after him, "You've been drinking the Kool Aid!" To which, the young man, ash still dripping off his forehead, replied cheerfully, "Just a little bit!" Six days later he was ordained in the One, Holy, Catholic and Apostolic Church! A classic example of ministerial leadership in post-Christendom Cascadia.

While self-identification as a Christian in Cascadia can bring you into contact with folks who might fit more easily in the "angry atheist category," these kinds of encounters are not as common as in other places where reaction against the church is still strong. A friend who recently moved to Quebec remarked about the hostility towards the church there, with the usual Quebecois secularity, compared to our more laid-back West Coast version of life without God. One day she casually invited a co-worker to attend a choral music concert at her church scheduled to take place the following weekend. Her colleague's face distorted in anger and said, "I will NEVER, ever enter a church—ever." Well, it makes sense then why swear words in Quebecois French are taken from the Roman Mass. *Les Canadiens de Montreal n'ont pas repris les eliminatoires—tabernack!* In Vancouver, our friend remarked people would shrug their shoulders and respond to the same kind of invitation instead with the "Vancouver maybe"—which essentially means a polite no.

Leadership in missional Christian communities here means coming to terms not so much with a culture of angry atheists, but rather the more commonplace "affable agnostic." West Coast author and artist Douglas Coupland famously claimed in his book *Life After God* that Generation X (now in our forties and fifties) were the first generation raised without religion in North America. Our experience is that it goes back even further with some people in Cascadia happily on their third or fourth generation raised without religion. So, what kind of leadership is required for effective Christian communities in this context?

The *Treasure in Clay Jars* project examined leadership through the lens of what they called "missional authority." For the authors, leadership and authority in missional communities is shared as "a community of multiple leaders, leaders who focus on missional vocation, leaders who foster missional practices, both new and from the tradition."[1] This emphasis on practices was central to the argument whereby leaders foster missional practices among their congregations. They suggested, "It is not enough for them to lead the congregation in good projects. If the congregation by its life

---

1. Barrett, *Treasure in Clay Jars*, 142.

together is to be a sign of the reign of God, leaders will encourage missional practices and hold people accountable for them."[2]

At first glance this is a helpful way to capture the changing nature of leadership. If Christendom encouraged people to "outsource their baptismal vows" to paid clergy, then a post-Christendom form of leadership would be empowering to all. Fear of dominant, charismatic and egotistical leadership led some in the church in North America to adopt the curious phrase, from the "sage on the stage to the guide on the side." Ken Evers-Hood echoes this when he stresses the importance of shared leadership at Tualatin Presbyterian Church in Portland. As mentioned in chapter 1, Ken has been committed to training up lay preachers in his congregation for years. Now, his church is a large, affluent suburban congregation. It doesn't *need* lay preachers because of a lack of ordained ministers or resources. Ken describes the worship style as "creative traditional." He writes, "I wear a robe, and we have a choir and a bell choir. We also have a thriving liturgical arts program. Recently, we installed temporary 'saints' into our windows: Howard Thurman, Dorothy Day, Harriet Tubman, Bonhoeffer, and Oscar Romero. These came down for Advent. Our art rules are nothing permanent, no words, and no felt."

Ken is committed to the work of raising up lay preachers because it is his style of missional leadership—equipping the saints for ministry. Not everyone makes the cut and he's clear on that. Some have a gift for preaching, others don't. To make room for lay preachers he gives away a Sunday each month to let someone else preach. He's there in worship, leading prayers and hosting other parts of the liturgy, but he yields the pulpit on purpose. Ken calls himself the "chief ball roller," saying, "I have a lot of ideas, but I bring them to our Session. I am never so pleased as when they push back and help an idea to shift and change." This equipping of the saints helps in the shared leadership model that Ken has developed over the years and that seems to fit the Cascadian context well. Ken notes, "Our community is also more Pacific Northwest than it is Presbyterian, meaning we are way more congregational. It wouldn't fly for me

2. Barrett, *Treasure in Clay Jars*, 146.

to tell folks what to think because I said so—I can tell them what I think, and then they expect to be listened to and heard. It's a fairly democratic and messy way of doing things, but I like it . . ."

Instead, Ken trains his laypeople to listen to the prompting of the Holy Spirit and tells them that you cannot preach unless you have a word from the Lord. He wants them to get out of their head alone (where good Presbyterians live!) and see proclamation of the Word as both cognitive and holistic. The training of his lay preachers is similar to how he approaches all the leadership offices in the congregation. He has all of his leaders—elders, deacons, lay preachers—go through a workshop he leads on writing their own statement of faith. At the end of the workshop, everyone has to stand up and read it out loud. No Christendom outsourcing of baptismal vows in Ken's church. The statements of faith are often raw, honest, vulnerable, and a gritty revelation of the risen Christ amongst God's people.

It's important to Ken's leadership that baptized Christians be able to articulate what is core to their relationship with Jesus. In this way he echoes fellow PC-USA colleague and missiologist Christopher James at Dubuque Theological Seminary, who has suggested to us here in the Centre for Missional Leadership that while "faith comes through hearing," preachers often overestimate the impact of their own preaching. His research and publication on church plants in Seattle offers ample evidence to back up his claim. James believes that faith also comes through "speaking" and that the speech act of faith needs to be both modelled and encouraged by church leaders. That's what Ken has been doing for years with the people of Tualatin Presbyterian Church. Ken says straightforwardly, "If I don't know what folks believe how can we work together? There's freedom here within demands, and a process of sharing deep, intimate and real stuff." Ken has taken this passion of equipping his members for their own leadership to the point of becoming a certified coach. Ken tells us, "I just finished a leadership coaching certificate and I'm working with our deacons to transform them from a more traditional caregiving/gossip model to a more coach-like model where deacons are being trained in deep listening to help members of their parish identify places in their life and faith in which they want to grow. I'm super jazzed about this." While our research in Cascadia did find healthy models of team leadership that took seriously the equipping of the "saints for ministry," most of the leaders, including Ken, also exhibited strong characteristics of apostolic leadership.

Many missional thinkers such as Alan Hirsch and Michael Frost have reminded us that post-Christendom leadership requires us to revisit Paul's offices of leadership in Ephesians 4:

> So Christ himself gave the apostles, the prophets, the evangelists, the pastors and teachers, to equip his people for works of service, so that the body of Christ may be built up until we all reach unity in the faith and in the knowledge of the Son of God and become mature, attaining to the whole measure of the fullness of Christ.

The APEST model of Apostolic, Prophetic, Evangelistic, Shepherding and Teaching ministries is one that can be particularly challenging for those seeking to lead formerly mainline Protestant denominations. Why? While Protestants have recently passed through the 500th anniversary of the Reformation, complete with Martin Luther playmobile figurines, the Reformation helped clarify "what kind of Christian you were," without ever questioning the dominant worldview that everyone in Latin Western Christendom was born already Christian. In that sense, the primary focus was on a teaching ministry for correct doctrine and a pastoral or shepherding role for those in the new folk or state churches or anabaptist communities. As John Calvin noted in his commentary on Ephesians 4,

> It should be observed, also, that, of the offices which Paul enumerates, only the last two are perpetual. For God adorned His Church with apostles, evangelists and prophets, only for a time, except that, where religion has broken down, He raises up evangelists apart from Church order (*extra ordinem*), to restore the pure doctrine to its lost position. But without pastors and doctors there can be no government of the Church.[3]

3. Calvin, *Epistles*, 179–80.

The concept that apostolic, prophetic, and evangelistic offices were no longer needed beyond the establishment of the early church reflects Calvin's own Christendom captivity. James Krabill and Stuart Murray have argued recently that the church's mission in Christendom was distorted by the loss of the first three offices of ministry. First was the loss of the apostolic function and calling whereby Christians in the Christendom period had little or no awareness of being sent. Second, in a society that was ruled by divinely authorized monarchs, there was no need for prophetic witness or campaigns for social justice. Third, in a world where almost everyone was Christian by birth within the territorial boundaries of a supposedly Christian society, evangelists and evangelism had no relevance.[4]

Calvin's warning of a time where religion might break down, sometimes translated as a "decay of religion," may be an apt description of the post-Christendom landscape. And as such, the resurgence of apostolic, evangelistic, and prophetic leadership is crucial. Many of the congregations we visited were either church plants, replants, or places of significant revitalization requiring apostolic leadership. But this does not mean a stand-alone, charismatic leader. For example, Albert Chu, pastor at Tapestry Church in Richmond, was clear that he made a decision early on as Tap began church planting out of their first site *not* to replicate himself. With each new church plant, Albert made the strategic decision to invest in the local campus pastor instead of drawing attention to himself. He reminded us that each campus pastor did the hard work of walking the neighborhood; meeting the local school principal, city planners, and politicians; and engaging the community associations. Instead of swooping in to preach in various neighborhoods, Albert sees his role as supporting the campus pastors, meeting every two weeks to check in, discuss preaching texts, read a book together, share their consolations and desolations while praying for a shared vision of what God is bringing. As Albert says, "My succession plan is that Tapestry doesn't replace me. That way when I go, the model goes and something new takes its place."

---

4. Krabill and Murray, *Forming Christian Habits in Post-Christendom*, 29.

Darrell Guder emphasizes the need for the recovery of the "sending" role of Christian community, rather than the more obvious "gathering" role the church played in Christendom. That we have no sense of "sentness" is evidence of the loss of missional vocation in the theology of the church and practice of faith in the world. Guder notes that when we enter church, together we put on the nametag "disciple" and sit at the feet of Jesus to be equipped for witness in the world. When we leave the Christian worship gathering, however, all together we flip the nametag over, so it reads "apostle" or sent ones. Leadership is about equipping every baptized believer for this ministry in the world. Guder argues,

> Missional leadership, centered upon the Word and practiced with evangelical collegiality, must serve the gathered church by preparing each member for his or her apostolate. However one calls it, the ministry of the laity, ministry in the workplace, Christian living Monday through Saturday, the presenting issue for the missional community is this: How do we equip each other to walk worthy of our calling in the personal apostolates into which God sends us every time we make the transition from gathered to scattered community?[5]

This equipping was something that Tim Dickau took to heart when he arrived as pastor to a small, elderly Baptist congregation in east Vancouver thirty years ago. There was an expectation that the best days of Grandview Church were behind them, cut off from the neighborhood with most worshipers commuting in for Sunday worship alone. Tim and his wife Mary moved into the neighborhood, however, and invited others to do so over the years ahead. Many of them shared homes (as did Tim and Mary) either with fellow church members or those in need in the community. Tim and Mary still live there thirty years later with one of their three sons and a daughter-in-law, as well as their grandson and many mealtime guests. They estimate that they have lived with more than thirty-eight people over the last thirty years and it has become a way of life for them. He describes this act of radical hospitality as flowing

5. Guder, *Called to Witness*, 159.

from his passion about widening our imagination for how we can be the church in a way that brings hope and transformation among both persons and societal structures in particular neighborhoods.

Here's the thing. It wasn't just the pastor doing this. Yes, Tim and Mary took the lead in modeling this form of incarnational missional leadership in the neighborhood. But over the years that followed others caught the vision and enacted this same model of missional engagement. Tim laughs when he describes how at first the highly secularized neighbors were suspicious of these "Christians" moving into the neighborhood to share life together. Somehow, having people drive in from other parts of the city for a once-a-week religious ceremony and then leave was one thing, but having people actually inviting you over for dinner was more unsettling!

Tim's book *Plunging Into the Kingdom Way* explores the story of the grace-filled and the difficult elements of the first twenty years of that journey. The book describes four trajectories the church moved towards including practices of radical hospitality, shared life among cultures, seeking justice for the least, and confession. In the last three decades, the church has found creative ways to bear witness to the good news of God's reconciling and restoring love through community living, welcome of the poor and the stranger, economic development through social enterprises, a twenty-eight-unit community housing project, proliferation of the arts, prophetic witness, and deepening practices of confession and repentance. Tim describes this transition as having moved from "going to church to *being* the church . . . in and for the neighborhood."

We have taken our students from St. Andrew's Hall and the Vancouver School of Theology to visit at Grandview Church over the years. Not only is it an inspiring and humbling example of a community shaped by a vision of missional leadership, but we always wait until a student raises their hand and asks, "How long did you have to work at this missional vision before you saw any fruit?" Nonchalantly, Tim will shrug his shoulders and say, "about ten years." The students are shocked by the answer. They hoped instead to hear that church revitalization happens quickly, with the right charismatic leadership! Instead, they gain a lesson on the curious nature of God's call, the need to root oneself in a community and wait and work patiently for the Holy Spirit to act. All important lessons of missional leadership itself.

Reflecting back with us on his thirty-year ministry at Grandview Church and the surrounding neighborhood, Tim says that a vow of stability is important. Two ways people can commit: a) you work through relational difficulties; b) you make important vocational decisions with other members of the community. Tim shares with us how even the difficult times that are inevitable in shared life together can be viewed as an opportunity for God to teach us more about God's nature and about our understanding of grace. "When things get difficult, we've learned how to lean in closer together, rather than move further apart," he says thoughtfully. This is the outcome of missional leadership in a post-Christendom context, according to Tim, a thicker description of shared life together in Christ.

As professors equipping the next generation of missional leaders, this patience, this stability, this willingness to serve in marginal spaces over decades—trusting that God is at work—can be hard for those entering ministry with dreams of large congregations and significant social impact. Father Matthew at Church of the Annunciation in Portland signaled the perils and pitfalls of these early years of ministry beautifully when he said, in the Orthodox tradition they have a saying: "When the priest is ordained for the first two years God *fears* the priest. Hopefully after that, the priest fears God!" Father Matthew reflected on how his early years of ministry brought many painful, humbling experiences that required his surrender of any messiah complex he had brought into ministry. He acknowledged the profound place of the Holy Spirit as teacher, quoting an Orthodox prayer directed to the third person of the Trinity, "O heavenly King, Comforter, Spirit of Truth Who art everywhere present and fillest all things, come and abide in us and cleanse us of all impurity and save our souls O Good One!" He reflected on the hard-earned lesson that nothing in worship or fellowship has more than earthly meaning without the activity of the Holy Spirit. This insight shaped his understanding of the Church as being "not of this world" but "in this world" and of the "age to come." Father Matthew noted that for Orthodox Christians their entire sacramental life is based on this perspective. He wrote, "The Orthodox Church (at its best) is never a thermometer of the times in which it lives, but rather a thermostat that constantly defines the temperature." These insights came to Father Matthew only after being brought to his knees and led through a deeper conversion, a pruning in which the Holy Spirit was his teacher. Missional leadership requires this kind of surrender in what theologian Andrew Purves calls the "crucifixion of ministry." Purves argues that there is nothing redemptive about our ministries, only the ministry of Jesus is redemptive: "Our people don't need us; they need Jesus. Our job is to bear witness to him, trusting that he continues to be the One who forgives, blesses, heals, renews, instructs and brings life out of death."[6]

Working on this project brought us into contact with so many remarkable, humble, effective missional leaders who could all articulate a similar process of long, stable leadership that brought them to their knees repeatedly in prayer making clear that it was God alone who was leading. Sitting in his office at Tenth Church Ken Shigemitsu shares how when he first arrived at the church it was going through a prolonged period of decline and isolation from its surrounding community. The revival at Tenth, now one of Vancouver's largest churches with multiple sites, is intimately tied up with Ken's own journey of deepening discipleship. Ken shares with us during those difficult early days of ministry at Tenth that God offered him a scriptural verse to hang onto, 1 Samuel 2:35: "I will raise up for myself a faithful priest, who will do according to what is in my heart and mind." This invitation to let go of the worldly concerns of "success" (too often found in the church as well!) and simply focus on being a faithful missional leader who would place first what was in God's heart and mind was life-changing for Ken, and for his ministry. He also reflects on a pilgrimage tour to Ireland with his mentor Leighton Ford, paid for by Ken's grandmother (who was sure a nice La-Z-Boy chair would have been a better use of the money). In Ireland, visiting various monasteries, Ken was

6. Purves, *Crucifixion of Ministry*, iii.

struck by the need for a rule of life. Upon return to Vancouver, Ken formed his own rule of life, to see and seek God not only in times of prayer but in *every* moment. Frequently going on silent retreat, he learned to enter into prayer more deeply and discovered that communion with God truly was the best and most intimate act of a human being, being human. Ken laughs, saying he finds silence even better than making love, sailing, or any other thrilling activity. Hearing Ken talk about that kind of connection with God explains both his tremendous impact as a missional leader and what others see in him that they want for themselves.

The missional leaders we experienced in the course of this work were highly intelligent pastor-scholars, committed to their church and community over the long haul, effective communicators of the gospel and motivators for others to follow in a similar self-sacrificing lifestyle. Perhaps most surprisingly, they were also ego-less leaders who were first and foremost deeply steeped in an intimate life with God: Father, Son, and Holy Spirit. The kind of missional leadership present in these people were those who could both discern (in community) the heart and mind of God for their context, and who had the courage and grace to enact that kingdom vision right where they are.

Questions for Reflection and Action

1. What is the most significant lesson God has taught you about leadership over the years?
2. How are you, and your community, equipping the saints in your midst for leadership in real and concrete ways?
3. What does it mean for you, and those in your community to walk worthily where you live, work, and play?

5

Craft Church

Seeking the Kingdom on Our Doorstep

It may seem odd to the uninitiated to speak of Cascadia as a region, especially if we include British Columbia. Governors on the West coast of the United States banded together during the COVID-19 crisis to say they three would decide when Cascadia reopened, and not the head of any other government. They should have called themselves "Southern Cascadia," for in real life, British Columbia is included. If Cascadia is even a thing, it crosses a national border, with significant differences on either side of the 49th parallel (don't call British Columbia "the Pacific Northwest" unless you want a polite Canadian correction!). Washington and Oregon have significant differences from one another—several pastors point out to us that Oregon was founded by more Confederate-leaning slaveholder-type pioneers, and Washington had more egalitarian beginnings. Each state and the province of British Columbia all see massive cultural differences between their urban coastlines and their more rural interiors.

Yet the parallels are just as plain. Weather and geography are similar—mountain ranges capture warm, moist air and keep the region temperate and very, very wet. Those trees are majestic for a reason—they are well watered. British Columbia, Washington, and Oregon each have more liberal and libertarian leanings politically than the rest of their countries (the libertarian leanings can go so far left they wind up on the right, of course). They tend to lead their respective countries in tech innovation and growth. Each has its own troubled history with race, as British Columbia interned Japanese-Canadians longer than the United States did and never returned their property, only apologizing to descendants in the 1980s. More recent immigration from Asia has brought money, a rich cultural mix, great food, and often unnamed tension. Perhaps you have heard of the "Seattle freeze"? In the Emerald City, folks might befriend you quickly and then ghost out and drop you just as quickly. It's on in Portland and Vancouver too. These are lonely, isolated, and isolating places. Tony Robinson, longtime Seattleite, jokes that the white stuff on the Rocky Mountains isn't just snow. It's the torn-up baptismal certificates of people moving west. The church's perennial weakness on this coast is both a cause and a fruit of social isolation. People don't want to go to church because they're isolated individuals. They're isolated individuals because they don't go to church. Easier to stay home and smoke (legal!) weed than deal with the pain-in-the-neck neighbor (or neighbour, if you're in Mr. Trudeau's country). As mentioned elsewhere in the book, Cascadia even has a flag. For real—look it up.

The churches in our study have responded well to these cultural challenges and many more. Each has found a way to have a posture of "yes" in response to its local neighborhood. In a region known for coffee and craft beer, each is a coffee and craft church. Some have grown big in the process, but they each maintain a personal touch. Each has to respond to vast disparities in the region between rich and poor, the over-housed and the under, while dealing with complicated real-estate situations of their own. Despite (or even because?) of the anti-hierarchical leanings in the region, each has to think through leadership with care. Each of these churches is also churchier than we might have expected. They don't eschew traditional teaching or practice, but they work hard to rethink it for a new and more skeptical day. And like craft brewers, they support one another. They don't compete with each other. Local beer places compete with Budweiser or Molson, not with the microbrewer on the same block. So too with these churches—not an ounce of competitiveness against other churches.

For example, pastor Elizabeth Ingraham Schindler arrived at Faith UMC in Issaquah, Washington, in 2014. She was unlike most of her predecessors. For one, she was a she. Faith was a church plant in the 1980s and had had all male pastors, and they were more conservative than most in the United Methodist Church in this region. They had all been on a retirement trajectory as they landed at Faith, given Issaquah is one of the priciest places to live in an obscenely pricey region. She was young—thirty-three years old. Suddenly this church of retired CEOs and lawyers had a pastor with bumper stickers on her laptop that read this way: "Not today Satan." And "All I need is a little bit 'o coffee and a whole lot of Jesus." On her introductory meeting at the church, Elizabeth observed that the drum kit could be sealed off and turned into a baptismal font. The engineer tour guides paused and wrinkled their brows. "I'm not sure it can be made water-tight," one said. "Engineers," Elizabeth thought, "I'm going to have to adjust my humor."

As she arrived, a tent city was ensconced on the church's lawn. Some of the region's homeless had found welcome among these nice Methodists and moved in for a spell. But the church's preschool did not feel well consulted. Many of the children have a mom in greater Seattle and a father back in Asia. New to a country and language and region, they did not all congratulate the church for its outreach to the poor, but rather withdrew their children from school. And not only the immigrant families. A money-maker became an instant problem. We asked Elizabeth how she dealt with this early "defeat." She corrected us. "I wouldn't call it a 'loss.' We're still in relationship with that tent city. Several come to church still." She reflected further. "If anything, we've learned from it. For example, our people phone first before they drop things off." The day after our visit, residents of the tent city are joining the church for dinner. Here we see how what could have been a volatile NIMBY and "us-versus-them" problem can become something more like a mutual relationship. Elizabeth had the personal experience and skill to frame the "issue" as an opportunity for growth: "These are my people; I get that they have problems that money cannot solve."

Jesus responds to our most difficult relational problems by setting a table in our midst and inviting people to sit together who never would otherwise.

Two churches in our study, Quest Church in Seattle and Tapestry Church in Richmond British Columbia, started life as majority-culture mainline churches. Quest's predecessor was Inner Bay Church, an Evangelical Covenant congregation—a denomination that was once called the Swedish Covenant. Tap's building once belonged to a Dutch congregation in the Christian Reformed Church—one of the two major Dutch Reformed denominations in North America. Both were aging white congregations in changed neighborhoods unable to reach their neighbors. In 2007, the intentionally multicultural Quest was renting from Inner Bay, when its senior pastor suggested, and the church agreed, to give their building away. Quest immediately became more multi-generational. It was young and multi-racial, but suddenly it also had an influx of older white people. Inner Bay's pastor served on Quest's staff for a time. Now, five of Quest's six pastoral staffers are women, four are people of color, and senior pastor Gail Song Bantum is a Korean-American who preaches like an African-American. It might be a circuitous route to inclusivity for a European denomination, but with courage and creativity it can be done.

Tap's founding pastor, Al Chu, was leading the English ministry at a Chinese Church in Edmonton but was frustrated. He wanted to lead in a missional way, but his congregation was not interested in relinquishing actual power. So, he took an opportunity from the Christian Reformed Church (CRC) to plant in Richmond. The parent CRC church offered Tap space for free for five years, the CRC denomination gave Tap six figures over five years (not a lot!), but then the congregation sold the building to Tapestry for $1 million when it could have gotten $4 million from developers. The property is worth many times that now. There were stipulations— Tap pays the former church's members a regular amount that they give away in the community. And we love this: Tap wasn't allowed to touch the pipe organ! But Tapestry has grown into a multi-site missional community that is some 70 percent pan-Asian and 30 percent all the rest of us. The church God is bringing to this region is notably different in complexion and culture than the "original" European settlers here.

Of course, even Europe is a bigger place than we sometimes imagine. Some of the earliest Christians in Cascadia came not from western or northern Europe but from as far east as you can get. Archaeological evidence suggests Russian Orthodox Christians may have been in California for centuries before Protestants ever arrived on this coast. Annunciation Orthodox Church outside of Portland follows in a long tradition of Orthodox missions up and down the west coast of the Americas.[1] Icons of St. Isaac of the Americas and St. Herman of Alaska crowd the interior of the space. The building itself suggests west-coastness. It was a log cabin-style church, built by a fundamentalist radio ministry. Father Matthew Tate *bought the building* with no land to put it on. Once land was procured it was broken into four pieces and moved to its present site in 1988. Now it feels like a retreat center as much as a church—with a duck pond and crops out back and an often fog-filled forest behind it. When some will say that Christianity is not indigenous to this region, Father Matthew will think to himself that actually he is doubly native. The Orthodox did not arrive recently and did not colonialize on western Europe's pattern. And his own grandmother was Chickasaw in Oklahoma, where Matthew was raised. Orthodox missionaries have had the resources to be more sensitive in relationship to aboriginal peoples in the Americas than Protestants were. The Orthodox believe in images, after all—it was Calvinists who cut down totem poles.

Father Matthew has the high cheekbones and flittering eyes and long, white ponytail that could have made him a celebrity in some other profession. And he once grew Annunciation by force of personality. He is a bridge figure. He unpacks well the Orthodox tradition in which he found himself as a convert. Former evangelicals looking for more mystery and antiquity often find it at Annunciation. He himself was working in hospice care with children dying of cancer and found "new age spirituality" had nothing to say. Orthodoxy did. Especially Russian Orthodoxy. When we

1. For more of this history, see Oleksa, *Orthodox Alaska: A Theology of Mission.*

notice that the icons at Annunciation seem to be weeping, he calls it the *nipsis* tradition in Russian Orthodoxy. They are seeing the mismatch between the world as God intends and as it is now. Plus, he says, Russians never miss a chance to suffer. "Greek Orthodoxy might be all fun in the sun, but in Russia we suffer in the cold," he said. His own charisma was not enough over the long haul, however. Inner-church conflicts, including over the place of Russian culture in an increasingly non-Russian church, led him to a breaking point. He heard God say that Annunciation did not belong to him, Father Matthew. He only worked there. "The Holy Spirit is the teacher here, and also the pruner here. I'm not a surgeon, but a midwife," he said.

Another Cascadian midwife is Tim Dickau, a sort of second founder of Grandview Calvary Baptist Church in Vancouver. Its location on the Drive in East Van has long been talked about among evangelicals as one of the most faith-adverse places in this highly faith-allergic city. But ask someone on Commercial Drive where to go to church and they'll likely point you to Grandview. As you'll hear throughout this book, however, Grandview Church does far more than worship. It works. One of its many social-justice initiatives is called just that—Just Work. It helps jobless people train to become social entrepreneurs in areas like pottery, catering, and renovation. Another is called Co:Here, a housing initiative for otherwise houseless people, built on the church's former parking lot with a good deal of city and provincial support. Grandview's preaching is a sort of stew of N. T. Wright and John Perkins—the inbreaking kingdom of God in Jesus meets our neighborhood where it most hurts, to bring healing. And not only in matters typically thought of as "religious." Dozens of Grandview folks live in around twenty intentional housing communities within walking distance of the church. Intentional Christian community is not first meant as a response to unaffordable housing. It is first meant to live in close proximity with difficult neighbors, not only one's friends. But what if what the church seeks—prayer—can dovetail with what the neighborhood needs—in this case, alternatives to unaffordable housing?

The leaders of the churches in this study are critical. They are all gifted, or their churches would not be thriving. Yet it is clear to each that she or he is not the point or reason or goal of growth. Each points elsewhere, and others notice. "Interested people are interesting," Pastor Ken Evers-Hood of Tualatin Presbyterian outside Portland tells us, echoing a seminary professor of his. And these leaders are *fascinating*, precisely because they are fascinated.

Take, for example, pastors Julia "Jules" Nielsen and Andy Goebel of Portsmouth Union Church in Portland who you first met in chapter 1. Pastor Andy was once a church planter with the same Evangelical Covenant to which Quest Church belongs. He trained in church planting, with a three-year formula of funding from headquarters before being weaned off and self-sufficient. The model had no local adaptability but was devised in Chicago to fit all times and places. And it worked. Goebel grew a little church. It was inclusive of LGBTQ+ people from the start, as befits this region. But the denomination tightened its conservative strictures and his previous church was suddenly looking for a new home. Meanwhile, Pastor Jules arrived at University Park United Methodist with a charge to decide within six months whether to close or continue. She was told University Park had some forty people. The number turned out to be closer to fourteen. Those who stuck around wanted to tear down the church and build affordable housing. But then Andy's refugees arrived. And suddenly a union emerged from two congregations and three denominations to make Portsmouth Union Church.

All of that denominational and polity rigmarole might matter more to pastors than to civilians. But this matters to all of Portland: there is no affordable housing in this region. The area is among the most desirable to live on the continent. New people are coming from all directions (most recently: IT workers priced out of the San Francisco Bay area, who find Portland "affordable"!). So, Portland's houseless community continues to mushroom. And PUC is responding. It has torn down a fellowship hall and made plans to build twenty units of affordable housing. "We wish we could do two hundred and fifty units," Jules said. "But this is the most we can do. What if twenty-five more congregations do the same?" she asks. The church has raised the money to build from a variety of public and private sources and is only awaiting city permits to go ahead. "We want to shift from building to being good neighbors," Andy said. PUC's neighbors may see Christianity as inherently oppressive, Trumpist, exclusive. But PUC's deep desire, desperation even, to give its property and money and energy away, may work toward changing that.

Agape Church of Christ has also found ways to serve its houseless neighbors. As mentioned in chapter 2, Agape is small—its pastor Ron Clark previously grew a big suburban church, but he found that approach facile and not particularly biblical. So now he's grown a small one—so small, in fact, that Agape closed during the course of this study. It never had land—it rented from a local high school—so how could it house anybody?

Pastor Ron Clark got to know residents of a homeless village near PDX airport and became part of a movement to replace tents with more semi-permanent wooden structures. Other community initiatives and churches heard about the tiny homes and offered land and resources and elbow grease to help. The city noticed this endeavor cost it no money and made it look good, so lent its blessing. Social workers and case workers could then find their clients. Rules and regulations could be established and more-or-less enforced. The village could elect its own leaders and practice democracy. Relationships can ensue. "If I can get someone into one of these villages, we can work on, say, their bipolar disorder, his doctor can find him, so can his church and community, so there's a three-pronged approach to help." Ron has taken the best can-do spirit of evangelicals and here blessed his city's most vulnerable population.

Ron is also a biblical scholar, with a PhD and regular practice of attending conferences and writing books. He has not served in an academic post, and so seems not to have had the love of learning ground out of him as so many of us have. He has written often about IPV—intimate partner violence—and presented what he has learned in secular venues. If he presents to Christians, he'll have a trickle of attenders. But if he presents to lawyers or politicians or law-enforcement, the room will be packed. They will often tell him of Christians accused of IPV who will pack courtrooms with supporters. Who supports the victims? The Bible does, Ron says. Evangelicals often have extensive international publishing networks, so one of Ron's books was translated into Russian. But Russians said they did not have IPV in their country (!). But a domestic violence prevention group in Portland found Clark and asked for his help. There are some 100,000 Russian emigres in PDX, with no religious literature in Russian condemning IPV. Clark had the books, unwanted in Russian. Portland police wanted it—because they had no religious literature in Russian describing IPV and trying to dissuade folks from it. None of this could have been planned—Clark's scholarship, its translation, or its help to women and police in the Russian diaspora in Cascadia. "These are God things," Clark said. "God defends the oppressed."

Union Church is located in what must be one of the strangest cities in the world. I don't mean Seattle—I mean the Southlake Union area of Seattle. Not twenty years ago it was a dilapidated old warehouse district by the water, with housing that was historic, but charmless. Today it is the home of a little start-up called Amazon. Block after block of skyscrapers house Amazon's techies and marketers and whatnot. Walking the area, one literally cannot move fast enough. There is always some young rich international person with a lanyard overtaking you. Those people want to be fed (expensively) and housed (even more expensively) but not necessarily entertained. "If you're an engineer far from home, you might never leave your apartment," pastor James B. Notkin told us. "You don't even need to set foot in a grocery store anymore." It's not like the church can knock on their door. They're locked in, up in those high-rises, John the Baptists for the rest of us during COVID-19.

Union Church, which you'll recall from chapter 3, finds itself nestled in the midst of this city within a city. But if you don't know it's there, you might miss it. There is no sign out front. Literally— none. The storefront is a chocolate shop, the back is a music venue. The former exists because Seattle has plenty of coffee shops already and James B. loves high-end chocolate. The latter exists because with gentrification there comes a dearth of gathering space. The venue is rented every moment the church is not using it. Then on Sunday mornings the community that constitutes Union Church worships. It is overrun with children. Out of some two hundred who come to worship weekly, seventy are children.

Did we say weekly? We don't mean weekly. We mean biweekly. Union Church worships as a corporate body every other week. On one off week, they go and intentionally serve somewhere in the community. On the other they meet in small groups, after a brief worship service. The goal is laudable theologically—the church exists only to serve the neighborhood, and disciplined small groups are as important to our faith as corporate worship. But the schedule also perfectly matches Cascadia. Seattle is the titular home of the Seattle Freeze—that nefarious social process by which you ghost out of friendships with no explanation. Folks in the PNW may earn well, may be on the cutting edge of tech and culture, but they are just plain bad at making and growing in friendships. Disciplined small groups help with that. So too does service. It shows that you make friends not by consuming together with similar people. You do it by going places not in the tourist guidebooks, making creative and risky friendships with those unlike you. James B. and Rene Notkin are wedded in marriage and ministry, come from University Presbyterian in Seattle, a long-time megachurch and creative incubator of such experiments as short-term mission trips (someone had to invent them—right?). But Union is a different way of doing church. Unlike UPC's prominent building on the University of Washington campus, Union Church blends into the neighborhood. Sitting with the pastor baristas in the crowded chocolate shop, without any evidence of a PC-USA congregation as owners, Renee muses, "When someone walks into this space that God has provided for us, how are they welcomed? While Jesus' name may never be mentioned, how is Jesus' living presence experienced?" At first, they rented nearby to launch Union in the neighborhood before falling into the opportunity to buy their current space, which architecturally is a hipster's paradise. Now they say "yes" as a default posture to every ask they can. They don't defend their space—they give it away. And they notice that the patrons of the chocolate shop pay attention to how they handle homeless and mentally ill patrons. "We keep a William fund," they said of one mason jar, stuffed with change for one regular. "We told William he can't panhandle, he can only ask us for money," they said. Every church has to set similar boundaries. But coffeeshop patrons pay particular attention to how Jesus's people relate to Jesus's beloved poor.

These churches each show particular care for their neighborhood. Cascadia is the land of craft beer and gourmet coffee. People don't go to malls anymore—those temples to universal consumerism. But they want to know their butcher by name. Instead of driving for the cheapest haircut imaginable, they'll pay double to walk to a nostalgia-peddling barber who serves you a craft beer while waiting. Union Church would look quite different if it were in a different part of Seattle—even a very *similar* part of Seattle like Ballard, Fremont, or Queen Anne. So too Tapestry Church in Richmond looks different even than quite similar growing multi-site churches elsewhere in the Lower Mainland. When Tap's building was maxed out, they looked at where their people were coming from. Quite a few were crossing the Arthur Laing Bridge after coming from all parts of Vancouver. So, they plotted a neighborhood to plant in. They rented a theatre in Marpole, where there weren't a lot of other churches. "Then we said, 'we never want to see you crossing the bridge again.'" Did you catch that? Vancouverites were *forbidden* from coming *to their own church*. They were, instead, to go to a new place, with the missional intention of forming Christian community and inviting neighbors. That church is now full as well, so too a third in a farther-out suburb. This is the opposite of the giga-church phenomenon—it is growing big by growing small. Splitting off, dividing, planting anew. Those who join Tap know they may be asked to pull up stakes and start anew elsewhere. It's discipleship, after all. Don't get too comfortable in any one place, or Christ will call you elsewhere.

We should notice some similarities across these churches in Cascadia. Each is attuned to the wider social problems in its neighborhood: houselessness, loneliness, rootlessness. Each is a custodian of its space in a way that seeks to say "yes" to weird asks, hoping to build community with new people. Each presents the gospel in local drag. Neighbors have heard Christians are hypocrites on poverty, social justice, and a myriad of other things. These churches present a quieter alternative where disciples actually try to live out Jesus's teachings in their flesh. Each holds out a gospel that is "for the healing of the nations," as Revelation says, longing for reconciliation between indigenous peoples, European settlers, Asian immigrants, and more recent Middle Eastern refugees.

And each shows us that the church is alive and well in Cascadia and can anticipate a future full of faithful creativity.

Questions for Reflection and Action

1. Some of these churches speak of their desire, their "desperation" even. What is your church desperate for?

2. To ask a question from Will Mancini, how is your church unlike ten thousand other churches?[2] How does it represent your local flavor, your block, your neighborhood? And how are those deep local roots a gift with which to do ministry?

3. Where does your neighborhood hurt (only one unacceptable answer: nowhere)? What sort of healing might Jesus bring precisely there?

2. Mancini, *Church Unique.*

6

Missional Metrics

Incarnational, Investment, and Intentionality

Standing at the backdoor of the sanctuary, the wedding guests cheerfully greeted one another as they made their way out, smiling politely at the minister, and spilling onto the front steps of the Vancouver church for a group photo with the happy couple. The wedding planner doubled back into the building, eyes darting around looking for any stray guests needed for the photo, lest her essential role go unnoticed. Noting the minister packing up she quipped, "Uh, thanks Reverend, that was great. Everyone seems to be happy. That's the important part, right?" Pausing a minute to look down at her clipboard and color-coded agenda for the day, she continued, "You know, our work is similar. We give people what they want and try to keep everyone happy." And with that vocational declaration, she disappeared out of the church in search of the photographer. Lord, have mercy.

Is that what ministry has become? Giving people what they want and trying to keep everyone happy? Does that not reduce pastoral leadership to Stanley Hauerwas's famous critique that most pastors today are little more than "quivering masses of availability?" Nevertheless, it raises an important question for Christian witness: What are the missional metrics to measure our ministries by? Christendom metrics were easier to spot and might be summarized by using the language of "noses, nickels and renown." How many people did you have in your church and how much money was coming in through the offering plates? As well, what was your church known for—the choir, the organ, the gym, a master "pulpiteer" or perhaps the finest acoustic and best architecture in town? Of course, it wasn't just the number of people in the pews, but what "kind" of people. Even to this day both of us guest preach weekly in churches across North America. A warning sign for us of a Christendom-era church is when someone in charge (minister or elder, for example) goes out of their way to point out to us as a guest who the "important people" are in the congregation. Seated at the front as worship begins, someone leans in close, as if to share a secret, whispering "That man in the third pew is a judge," or "the woman coming up to read Scripture is a surgeon," or "the person introducing you this morning is the CEO of a big business here in town." Who cares? Their position, prestige or financial success is not telling us much about their discipleship to the Lord Jesus Christ. In fact, it might actually best be said as caution, not celebration. Whenever this happens you can almost hear Jesus's encounter with the rich young ruler, where the Lord looked on the man with love but warned, "One thing you lack: go and sell all you possess and give to the poor, and you will have treasure in heaven; and come, follow Me."[1] In churches like these, Christendom metrics of "success" are still deeply ingrained. There is an awareness that they are in trouble as leaders note the dwindling numbers in the pews (with special attention to counting the powerful or prestigious parishioners) and cling to the financial health of the congregation and its investments for a sense of value into the future. As well, these congregations still long for standing in the public arena, as well as within the denomination—"we're a tall steeple church." The historical or architectural significance of the church building itself (our organ is bigger than yours!) and quality of the music program were also part of the reputation or renown of the congregation in the community

1. Mark 10:21.

in years past. Needless to say, the metrics of effective ministry from the past have not fared well in the transition to post-Christendom. However, there are many still within the declining, historic "euro-tribal" denominations in North America who still think in these terms of metrics and reward clergy who also share these values. So, if these metrics are no longer helpful, then what might be?

In our site visits, interviews and study of missional congregations across Cascadia there were significant clues emerging regarding how these Christian communities were evaluating their own faithfulness to the gospel. It's important to note, however, that new missional metrics does not mean necessarily having to reject outright the former metrics of Christendom. In fact, missional metrics can take the traditional measures of "effectiveness" and transform them from noses, nickels, and renown to *incarnational, investment, and intentionality.*

First, *incarnational engagement.* Yes, people matter. You could even go so far as to say that numbers matter. After all, behind every number is a person that Jesus died to save and enlist in God's reconciling mission for the healing of the nations. The story of Gideon in the book of Judges offers us a key insight, when God reduces the number of warriors, saying, "The troops with you are too many for me to give the Midianites into their hand. Israel would only take the credit away from me, saying, 'My own hand has delivered me.'"[2] Whether large or small in number, the question is whether the focus is on divine agency at work, rather than relying on the strength, influence, and worldly power of the church's membership. Indeed, if we affirm that people matter then that means that *everyone* has shared value, not just those who hold positions of power and prestige. Once again, a missional understanding of engagement returns to "The Word became flesh and blood and moved into the neighborhood."[3] Note, the translation does not say that the Word became flesh and moved into the church. The incarnation of the Son of God into the world means that we are to look for God's activity everywhere around us, *and* in everyone—whether Christian

---

2. Judg 7:2, NIV.

3. John 1:14, MSG.

or not. A missional incarnational metric acknowledges that people matter, all people in the neighborhood. Ron Clark, who we've already met several times in earlier chapters, reminds us of that in Portland with his emphasis on counting conversations, rather than conversions. His ministry that includes sex workers and homeless in the downtown core has focused on building deep relationships and broader community support, including many who would not self-identify as Christians. Ron sees a glory being returned back to God through that. As the gritty reality of the fallen world is exposed, people's humanity is laid bare, and our need for God's grace and transformation becomes evident. Ron reflected on how in the fallen culture around us society endorses arresting prostitutes yet glorifies the pimp's lifestyle. "We too often blame the victim rather than empower them," Ron says pausing to think, "We need to ask guys why you can't learn to look at women in healthy ways? That's hard to do!" He likes the language of "missional-incarnational" giving a nod to Alan Hirsch and Michael Frost, noting that what bothers him the most is that too many churches see "missional" as sitting around discussing mission. He hears from people on the streets in downtown Portland that Christians, especially clergy, are not engaged in the community. Ron says, "My take would be that we need leaders to go into the community, serve alongside agencies, develop relationships with all people, become a voice in the city, and lead our people to follow. When we do that, we invite marginalized voices to the table and hear their perspectives on the biblical narratives. It helps us to become incarnational." Ron adds that he believes what we do for Jesus today shows that the reign of God is here—active and present. Our role is to participate with the Holy Spirit in calling people to the Kingdom.

A little further north in the city of Portland at Portsmouth Union, Jules Nielsen and Andy Goebel have watched a new church form out of a commitment to seeing God present in all the people of their community. As you first read in chapter 1, Andy moved down from Washington state originally to plant a church but his clear commitment to inclusion of LGBTQI people put him at odds with his former denomination. Asked to leave, he was introduced to Jules who pastored a small United Methodist congregation in the hardscrabble neighborhood of Portsmouth. Originally a stand-alone suburb of Portland, the community had been absorbed years earlier and struggled to retain its own identity. Jules was early in her ministry with the United Methodist congregation, small in numbers and struggling to discern how to connect with the neighborhood facing such obvious need. When introduced to Andy, the two leaders hit it off right away, even though they come from very different backgrounds. Together, they feel they model a way of being church that creates space for difference and understanding. Sitting down to talk with them, it is obvious they play off each other's strengths and made it clear that they have a commitment to always speak plainly. Jules says, "You better be ready to be called on your shit. We've developed a culture of direct communication—a sense of urgency in what needs to be done and so there is no patience in toxic church culture." That commitment extends to the whole community, not just the leadership, where people need to be on board with the values of the mission and participate in the ministry to, and with, the neighborhood. When their two communities began worshiping together, they identified their shared values, which included hospitality, inclusion, and openness in the words and ways of Jesus. This led to a commitment to the neighborhood that included many homeless people faced with the issues of drug addiction and mental health. The day we met with them the sanctuary was set up with a hundred cots ready for the evening shelter. The church had leaned into not only addressing the needs of an emergency shelter with plans for affordable housing, but with a posture of curiosity about what God was teaching them in and through the neighbor they served. Jules and Andy describe the Holy Spirit showing up every week when this varied community of homeless and neighborhood families comes to the Communion table as one in Christ. Together, they're learning that a people who engage in vulnerability, direct communication, and mutual service are demonstrating the work of God. It's not a church that is driven by programs, but rather with a focus on ministering to people and attending to the presence of Christ in their midst.

On the south side of Portland, in the suburb of Tualatin, Ken Evers-Hood notes how the youth of his congregation were committed to connecting with their Hispanic neighbors (many of whom worked on farms just outside Portland). In 2018, Tualatin Presbyterian Church was one of twelve congregations selected to receive a $15,000 grant and participate in The Log College Project of Princeton Theological Seminary, an initiative centered around creating, testing, and implementing new models of youth ministry. Through this program the youth from Tualatin Presbyterian Church have been building friendships with Hispanic youth who live in nearby apartment buildings through a "Dreamer-sicle ministry." Children's minister Sarah Beck describes it this way: "Kids from our church and community partners gather in our shared space and make paletas, a Salvadorian dessert that is half ice-cream and half popsicle. On the stick will be written the words 'Working Together; Dreaming Together.' Our slogan is 'Dreamer-sicles frozen ice-cream desserts make I.C.E.[4] something sweet.'" This bridge-building ministry is meant to recognize and strengthen the relational connections between neighbors with a commitment to being in solidarity and counting all people, not just those in the church (or the more select members with prestige and influence).

Just as the Christendom metric of people (bums in pews) is still important if interpreted through a missional lens (humanity as a source of God's on-going revelation and participation in reconciliation), so too can the question of finance be re-interpreted. The "Nickels of Christendom" becomes instead *community investment*, in other words, the effectiveness of churches is not measured by how much money they have in the bank, or if they've managed to meet budget for another year, but how they steward their resources for the betterment of the community around them.

Grandview Church in east Vancouver offered us many examples of this kind of community investment. Today, Grandview Church has about fifteen community houses for church members, including clergy. That's partially driven by economics as the neighborhood gentrifies, but Tim Dickau also recognizes that the gospel challenges our "autonomy and individualism toward shared life and hospitality." This kind of close quarter engagement with neighbors

---

4. Immigration and Customs Enforcement, United States Government department.

creates important challenges for discipleship. As Tim notes, "when you can't stand someone that's the place where love is taking place, where we meet God, where the work of discipleship truly begins." Over the course of thirty years engaging the neighborhood in mission, the church developed, refined, and committed to the following four visionary trajectories, moving:

1. from isolation to community towards *radical hospitality*;
2. from homogeneity to diversity towards *shared life* among cultures;
3. from charity to friendship towards *seeking justice* for the least;
4. from the confrontation of idolatries to repentance towards *new life in Christ*.

One of the many ways Grandview has leaned into and lived out this commitment involves the development of the Co:Here housing project as noted in earlier chapters. Recognizing the affordability crisis in Vancouver (a similarity found in both Seattle and Portland throughout this study), Grandview Church worked for years building a coalition of community partners and government agencies. In this way, Grandview Church also illustrates the first transformation of a metric from "noses" to "incarnational engagement," by valuing people not based on their contribution to the church, but by their image bearing of God in the broader community. Care for all their neighbors, and relationships with them, led the congregation into such varied social enterprises noted in early chapters such as JustPotters, JustCatering, and JustRenos—successful pottery studio, catering, and renovation businesses that employ people in the community who face barriers to work including addiction, physical limitations, and mental health challenges.

These commitments to seeing the value in all their neighbors over several decades led Grandview Church to make a sacrificial investment in the community by donating a piece of land valued at $2.68 million near the church for the sake of affordable housing. Stop and think about that for a moment. Can you imagine a congregation steeped in Christendom memory and values, which can barely meet budget and yearns for a lucrative investment portfolio, giving up a piece of property worth nearly $3 million not for their own benefit, but for homeless and low-income neighbors around them? That's the transition from nickel counting to investment through a missional lens.

Rallying a diverse set of partners including Street to Home Foundation, the City of Vancouver, Canadian Housing and Mortgage Corporation, Salsbury Community Society, and the Canadian Federal Government, Grandview Church invested in their local community, providing shelter and a safe home for their neighbors on the streets. Completed in 2018 after a $11.9 million capital campaign, Co:Here has twenty-six self-contained units: eighteen studios for people who are homeless or are at risk of being homeless, four one-bedroom and four two-bedroom units for low-to-moderate-income individuals, couples, and families. The building design recognizes that space shapes engagement with people and as a result includes large indoor and outdoor community engagement spaces. Co:Here describes itself as being founded on the conviction that people are made for community. Co:Here brings together people from different economic backgrounds in a mutually transformative, supportive, and nurturing environment that allows vulnerable people to flourish. Residents journey together based on the principles of simplicity, community, respect, empowerment, and sustainability.[5] Commenting on the completion of the project Vancouver Mayor Gregor Robertson said, "Co:Here is a great example of the type of creative affordable housing solutions that are possible when all levels of government and our non-profit partners work together to deliver urgently needed housing."[6]

This recognition of the church's role in society by the political elites is just what a Christendom metric craved (renown), however, seen through a missional lens we can see the deep relational investment required with all neighbors (from the powerful to the least of these) in order to have that recognition today. Indeed, missional metrics can also embrace the former Christendom focus on the reputation of the congregation in the wider world. The question becomes, "What are you known for?" This might be a starting place

5. http://coherehousing.com.

6. "Unique Affordable Rental Housing Project," para. 5.

for congregations in post-Christendom if they are wanting to have an honest self-diagnostic. Don't ask "church people" but ask people who live in the community not connected to the congregation, "Hey, you know that church on the corner by the gas station, what is it known for?" The answers will be telling. We can think of a church in our area that would expect people in the community to answer (using the old Christendom metric of renown), "that's the church with the wonderful music program" given their million-dollar pipe organ and multiple paid soloists in the choir loft. However, when asked almost every community member replied, "Oh, that's the church that has the big flea market." The flea market that decades ago gave away all of its proceeds to mission and today keeps all of it for the operating budget. Hmm. But renown can take on a different meaning through a missional lens.

The missional communities we visited all seemed committed to developing a thicker sense of community life together. They were focused intentionally on their shared life together, rather than the reputation or renown of the church. James B. and Renee Notkin at Union Church, Seattle describe it as an emphasis upon relational theology that valued people not programs. "It's not just about getting to heaven. It's about living your life to the audience of One, grace-orientated rather than achievement-orientated. Faith as an adventure. It involves small group ministries where people really know each other—warts and all—and giving ministry away so that everyone shares it. It can never be egotistically driven." They reflected on how the whole community was excited and celebrated when they saw other people taking steps towards faith in Jesus. The thicker the community, the more excitement at risk-taking for the sake of God and neighbor asking, "What is God going to do in this world?" As Renee said, "When you say Yes to Jesus you say Yes to Jesus' people whoever they are . . ." This thickened community of disciples living and sharing life together becomes its own witness.

This missional metric of intentionality finds resonance in the imperatives of 1 Peter that call on Christians who find themselves as "strangers and exiles"[7] to "walk worthily" in the world. This call

---

7. 1 Pet 2:11.

to right conduct in the world as witness is not all tipped towards human agency, since the "strangers and aliens" are living as part of Christ's resurrected life and body in the world. In that sense missiologist David Fitch connects our walking worthily as Christians to our attention to Christ's presence not only in worship (where Christ is host and we are recipients), or in our homes (where we are hosts and neighbors are recipients of hospitality), but also in the wider community and neighborhood where we go open-handed, without power, as guests seeking Christ's presence. Intentional Christian community forms and shapes us to attend to the presence of Christ in the church, home and wider world. This is not easy, however, as Fitch comments:

> God's presence is not always obvious. He requires witnesses. God comes humbly in Christ. He so loves us, he never imposes himself on us. Instead he comes to us, to be with us, and in that presence he reveals himself. In his presence there is forgiveness, reconciliation, healing, transformation, patience, and, best of all, love. In his presence he renews all things. Presence is how God works. But he requires a people tending to his presence to make his presence visible for all to see.[8]

Placing this sacred role of "tending to God's presence" at the center of our common life together switches the Christendom metric of renown (look at our important church!) to the formation of an intentional people marked by baptismal waters, re-fashioned by the Word and nourished by the Lord's supper before being sent into the world. We saw this commitment again and again in the Christian communities we visited, and it was especially present from the founding of Tidelands Church north of Seattle on I-5 in Washington State.

The PC-USA congregation in Marysville, Washington (outside Everett), commissioned their youth pastor Brandon Bailey and his family, along with a handful of other families to begin a new witnessing community further north in the town of Stanwood, Washington. Buying a home on nearby Camino Island, Brandon and the

---

8. Fitch, *Faithful Presence*, 27.

families did not make the typical assumption of church planters (or new clergy to an established church!) that nothing of value had taken place before they arrived in the area. Instead, Brandon said that "We recognized that Jesus was already present and working in the Stanwood/Camano Island community." They made a commitment to establishing their presence first in missional communities. Brandon recalls that God initiated this church planting process, and their task was to try and connect with where the Spirit was moving and leading to be involved deeper in people's lives. Brandon said, "The purpose of starting this new church community was to share the love of Jesus and his good news with people by living our lives on mission: pouring ourselves out in service and love, building relationships, and providing an environment where all followers of Jesus can grow and live out their faith."

Meeting on Sunday nights in people's homes over a meal, the missional communities were designed to have core leaders (two or three per group) and focus on inviting people into relationship, introducing newcomers to Jesus through intentional daily living in a community that practices hospitality and open faith discussions. The communities strived to include key components such as being incarnational, service-orientated, intentional community for prayer and support, open to newcomers in the community, gathered around meals and breaking bread, aiming for multiplication to avoid stagnation, and setting prayer and Scripture at the center of their gathered life together. They placed an emphasis upon really getting to know their neighbor, practicing a ritual of setting aside their program over dinner if another member was courageous enough to invite a newcomer. Instead, the community would break bread and genuinely get to know more about who this new individual or family were. The gift of presence, hospitality, and listening offered to newcomers in these missional communities was something not found anywhere else in the broader community. And it helped them grow not only in numbers but in a thicker sense of shared life together. When is the last time you've had a group of people in your local church sit for an hour attending to your life story and asking supportive questions?

Reflecting back on the last eight years, Brandon notes how easy it is simply to go to "a few big moments in the life of our missional communities where we responded to the needs at one elementary school with the love of Jesus. Those moments didn't just happen—they came through many intentional hours of service. Hours volunteering in schools, serving on the PTA, listening to teachers and administrators, coaching kids in sports, praying." Looking to the future he adds, "Then imagine that multiplied by ten years, or twenty years! This is the vision and the dream that we have for Tidelands Church. And not just for those participating in our Missional Communities. Our hope is that everyone will begin to seek out how they can be the hands and feet of Jesus to those around them." Reflecting on key Scripture for the thickening of the intentional communities, Brandon does not go to the usual Acts 1:8 or Luke 10 passages espoused by many in the missional conversation but instead he offers, "Someone might claim, 'You have faith and I have action.' But how can I see your faith apart from your actions? Instead, I'll show you my faith by putting it into practice in faithful action."[9]

This thickening of intentional community through home groups meeting on Sunday nights and the full community in worship in Stanwood on Sunday mornings is designed for impact on the broader community. Brandon shared Tidelands' ongoing commitment to equip people to live out their discipleship in the workplace. He talked about the member of his church who works at SeaTac Airport for Homeland Security and who was equipped to start and lead a Bible study for fellow government workers. Or the schoolteacher who was given spiritual disciplines for being Christlike in the workplace where she could not name Jesus. Brandon says, "At the heart of the vision for Tidelands Church is the dream of being a church that will help people live the entirety of their lives on mission in the places where they already live, work, and play." This has been a distinctive mark of the church plant from the beginning. "We have never aspired to be a big program-oriented church, or an attractional church that will draw

9. Jas 2:18.

in large crowds on Sunday morning," says Brandon. "Rather, we have dreamed and hoped of being a church that will equip people to be disciples who make disciples—living faithful lives following Jesus in the stuff of ordinary life."

Albert Chu at Tapestry Church in Vancouver has also worked with his leadership team to form a thicker description of shared life together. This commitment to becoming more intentional as a community involves both incarnational and attractional elements according to Chu. The incarnational is the being present with and for neighbors in the world. This comes in a variety of ways, including a trailer available to any church member that includes a bouncy castle, kid's games, a BBQ, and a sound system, so that they can set up a block party for their neighbors throughout the summer. There is no overt promotional material from the church distributed, it is designed primarily to build relationships between church members and their neighbors. But a thicker community is also attractional, according to Chu. If Christians are walking worthily in their communities, loving and blessing neighbors, then there should be a desire to have others share that common life in Christ together with the invitation to "come and see." At Tapestry, Chu estimates 60 percent or more of the members are involved weekly in small groups. "That's where the pastoral care happens," he says, noting that the accountability and intentionality of thicker community is rooted in these groups, rather than a Sunday morning worship experience.

Missional metrics are replacing old Christendom values in many of these new and renewed witnessing communities across Cascadia. Of course, Christians have always measured their faithfulness and impact on the world around them. Once baptized, Christians are called to grow in holiness or sanctification as a sign of God's ongoing redemption and renewal of a beautiful, yet broken creation. Through *incarnational* presence with neighbors, *investment* in the community (without a myopic focus on the benefit to church) and through a commitment to thicker shared life together in *intentional* practices of discipleship making, Christian witness is operating from a new scoresheet. And the difference is refreshing.

Questions for Reflection and Action

1. How do you, and your community, measure effectiveness in ministry?
2. How are you sharing life with those outside of your church and investing in the community?
3. What does your church do to help equip people to attend to the presence of the triune God in their daily lives?

7

Catechesis and Coffee Hour Confession

B y the metrics of Christendom, the mainline church in Cascadia was doing well with good Sunday attendance, a strong children and youth program, a cherished choir stacked with paid soloists, powerful and influential congregants from business, medicine, and government, and lots of money in the bank. A young woman was new to the community and decided to join in the Sunday worship. She found a place in a pew and after worship even summoned the courage to enter the fellowship hall for coffee and stale cookies. She introduced herself to a number of people and stopped by the church's welcome table for some information. Meeting the clergyperson on the way out from the fellowship hall, she was warmly greeted and thanked for attending worship for the first time. When asked for her impressions as a visitor the young woman paused thoughtfully, hesitating as if deciding whether to be polite or honest. "Well, it was fine," she said quietly. "The only thing was I tried multiple times in coffee hour to talk to people about the worship. You know, like to discuss the theme of the day, or some of the good questions you raised in your sermon." She paused, sizing up the clergyperson's response thus far before pushing all her chips to the center and saying, "Every time I tried to talk theologically with people, they switched instead to talking about the weather or what they were going to do with the rest of the day. I guess I'm just used to a church where people want to talk about God." Ouch.

In the Christendom-era church, there were certainly ways that people were educated about the Bible, creeds, and church doctrine. Sunday schools, youth groups, and confirmation class were all expected of the young, and then after their teen years somewhat regular attendance in Sunday worship as adults, with optional Bible studies or other programs, became the norm. Alongside the churches' catechetical work with the young, the broader society helped reinforce these Christian norms with Bible readings and prayers in the public schools, Gideon Bibles handed out like candy at Halloween, politicians consulting church leaders and invoking the name of God with ease, and the rhythm of public life in sync with the church calendar from Sundays as a day of rest (no shopping!) and high holidays like Christmas and Easter given special designation in the broader culture. But it was not always this way.

Early church leader Tertullian once declared that "Christians are made, not born." And yet since the Emperor Constantine's fourth-century embrace (or perhaps domestication?) of the Christian movement, Christians were actually *born, not made*. But it was not always so. Our Christian ancestors in the early church took catechesis seriously. In fact, the "seeker-sensitive" services of the 1990s appear polar opposite to the practice of the early Christians. No, as Alan Krieder reminds us in *The Patient Ferment of the Early Church*, the church was careful about who it let into its worship time and limited participation depending on one's commitment level. Those who were sponsored into the church and began catechesis, known as catechumens, were only allowed to be present for the opening part of worship. Once the service of the Word was complete with readings and sermon, they were dismissed and only baptized Christians (and those with letters of recommendation from other churches) remained for the sharing of the Eucharistic meal.[1] Of course, we live in post-Christendom times, not in pre-Christendom. Our Christian witness has passed through, and has been indelibly marked by the fifteen-hundred-plus-year experiment of Christendom, where Christianity went from being a sporadically persecuted religious tradition across the Roman Empire (estimated by some scholars to be around 10 percent of the population) to the official state religion by the year 381. While relieved by the end of persecution, and even wooed by the possibilities of access to state power and resources, church leaders may not have realized how much was lost in this transition from persecuted minority to the religious arm of the state. As Christendom developed over several centuries, it eventually became taken for granted that one was born, lived, and died within a so called "Christian society."

But now in a post-Christendom context like Cascadia, churches are quickly discovering that if the culture no longer helps make the Christian, the work of former disciples is rightly back in the hands of the local church. This is especially evident in Cascadia with its strikingly high levels of secularity and non-church involvement. Over a hundred years ago, in 1914, Professor E. J. Klemme remarked in Washington state, "In the east they were faithful church members; now they are not even church attenders. The ascent of the Great Divide seemed too steep for church letters. The air of the Northwest seemed too rare for prayer. We have hurried forth to conquer the wilderness, but we have been conquered by it."[2] The struggle to either keep people committed to the church, or to make new disciples in this Cascadian soil has deep roots in this region. This process of "making disciples" is known as catechesis. From the Greek word κατηχέω (*katecheo*)—meaning to sound the echo—it is used, in part, to refer to the process adults went through in the early church prior to baptism, being asked several questions based on the baptismal creed and their response or echo of the teaching, affirming what they learned and practiced in catechesis.[3] This active and urgent shaping of "human beings being human" with

---

1. Kreider, *Patient Ferment of the Early Church*, 11.

2. Killen, "Introduction," 9.

3. Osmer, *Teaching Ministry*, 27.

a desire to be more like Jesus is picked up in Rick Osmer's definition of catechesis being "an interpretative activity undertaken by
congregations and their individual members who see themselves as
participants in the Theo-drama of the triune God and are seeking
to better understand their roles in this drama by deepening their
understanding of Scripture and Christian tradition."[4] And yet, Patricia O'Connell Killen has highlighted the particular challenge for
this identity making and shaping in a region like Cascadia where
the broader culture does not support such formation. Killen notes
the prevalence of those she calls "secular but spiritual" in the region
who either identify loosely with a religious tradition, or the growing category of "nones," including those who are overwhelmingly
not atheistic in worldview, but are simply ambivalent to the role
of religion in everyday life. With environmentalism as the default
civil religion for the "nones," they are formed by the values of care
for creation and "what it means to be fully human and part of the
region's ecosystem."[5]

Jessica Duckworth notes the dangers of an anemic approach
to discipleship and catechesis across the continent when arguing,
"This happens because there is not distinction between the cultural
practices of Christianity established in North America per se and
Christianity practiced within a particular congregation."[6] Essentially, she is asking a question important to every church in Cascadia
today: How do you make a Christian when the culture no longer
forms even a basic "cultural Christian" through Sunday School, a
vague knowledge of Jesus's atoning death, or a sense of obligation
to attend church maybe at Christmas or Easter? If the culture no
longer assists in forming a basic Christian identity, what are the
specific steps required to help an adult move from a pre-baptismal
to a post-baptismal identity in Jesus Christ? Duckworth profiles
congregations that are creating low-barrier/high-expectation communities of faith where non-Christians are warmly welcomed but
where catechesis can take years before the person is ready to shed

4. Osmer, *Teaching Ministry*, 237.

5. Killen, "Introduction," 18.

6. Duckworth, *Wide Welcome*, 24.

their happy pagan or affable agnostic cultural identity for baptism in Jesus Christ. According to Duckworth, the catechumenate provides a distinguishing mark in an otherwise indistinguishable posture of Christianity within Christendom, it is countercultural, by which she means, it is "the posture of the people under the cross . . . to be a movement that engages the world with suffering love."[7]

However you approach the topic, in post-Christendom Cascadia we are well beyond the traditional "Christian Education" program that often felt like it served to edify the Elect, an optional exercise of betterment like learning bits of a foreign language before overseas travel or taking an art class on a whim. No, discipleship formation for new or mature Christians is essential in a world that is increasingly either ambivalent or hostile to the Lordship of Jesus Christ.

An awareness of the importance of catechesis was evident in the churches we visited in Cascadia, even if they weren't sure if they were doing a particularly good job. Ken Shigematsu at Tenth Church confesses, "We are strong on welcome on the front end, we need to make better steps on catechesis." Gail Song at Quest Church acknowledges their attempt to go deeper with baptized Christians in order to form resiliency in them for life in a secular Seattle landscape. Song said, "Look, some churches baptize hundreds of people a year but can only go so deep with new Christians. I like to think of it as bigger square feet, but more time spent in the shallow end. Instead, we can go deep and have classes on hermeneutics, how to read Scripture, preach on subtle aspects of faith." She observes that those "other churches" are often a great place for people to be introduced to the Christian faith but that Quest was investing more in the lifelong development of disciples. She said, "We have been encouraging small-group Bible reading through a program called Immerse over the past two and a half years—primarily encouraging folks to read in diverse groups to gain broader ways of reading and interpreting Scripture. Overall, we have a community filled with folks from all faith and cultural traditions which inevitably informs their understanding of Scripture." Song pauses

---

7. Duckworth, *Wide Welcome*, 26.

before saying reflectively, "We're trying to be an imperfect church wanting to be faithful." Catechesis sounds a lot like that too. Father Matthew in Portland acknowledges the challenge of taking non-Christians and leading them through a process where they could participate fully in the ancient liturgy and embrace the theology of the Orthodox Church in a fast-paced North American context. Catechesis for them began with the honest realization that most people in his church grew up being told, "they could do whatever you want. It's not wrong," he notes, "it's just more American than Christian." He says that it is about immersing them in a deeper tradition, "We are Eucharistically centered. Everything comes out of that focus. The Orthodox Church has a rich and beautiful tradition of Feasts, Fasts, celebrations, funerals, spiritual practice, and sacramental initiation. We make every effort to remember *why* we do these things, not just how." Father Matthew illustrates the challenge of catechesis in a post-Christendom world. Following Jesus involves obedience to him and the way of life the gospel demands. This means we are being shaped to be counter-cultural often within churches that thrived on being respectable and mainstream in society. What if following Jesus sets you at odds with your family, neighbor, employer, or government when it comes to nationalism, immigration, human sexuality, care for the poor, medical assistance in dying, or how to spend your money? For those who are paying attention to catechesis as formation in a post-Christendom society, it is important to note that this work is not being done in a vacuum.

Bryan Stone argues that we live in a "culture of conversion" where in "every direction we turn, we are offered the promise of 'makeover', whether of body, face, wardrobe, career, marriage, home, personality, or soul."[8] The only question is who or what will convert your heart, mind, and soul? Stone argues,

> conversion is much more than an individual's deciding to believe new pieces of information that she or he now possesses. It occurs at the level of one's convictions, which . . . are so central to one's character as a person

8. Stone, *Evangelism after Christendom*, 258.

> that a change in them would involve a change (would,
> indeed be a change) in that person's character . . . In
> conversion, the whole person is remade—heart, mind,
> body, relationships, allegiances, habits. In essence, a new
> identity is acquired.[9]

Evangelism, evangelization, and catechesis help people to take steps towards faith in Jesus. For churches in post-Christendom, it is a wakeup call to realize that the formidable formation forces of the wider culture through media, marketing, and social norms are at work on our church members for the majority of their week, long before they walk into our Sunday service or mid-week small group. This is a particular challenge when the shaping of the world has been experienced as harm or trauma.

Ron Clark in Portland reflected with us on his catechetical work in downtown Portland with a wide variety of people the church pretends not to see. As noted earlier in chapter 2, he shares stories of Bible studies with sex workers seeking to leave the industry. Ron led a formation group for Christians who survived abuse of various kinds. They read the book of Exodus together, and through their survivor's eyes Ron heard new perspectives on the wilderness wandering of the people of Israel that he had never considered before. He is now trying to form relationships with those who bear painful stories of being evicted for not paying the rent, moving from low-income housing to low-income housing. They seize on Jesus's rebuke of the outwardly powerful and upwardly mobile, "they . . . love to be greeted with respect in the marketplaces and have the most important seats in the synagogues and the places of honor at banquets. They devour widows' houses and for a show make lengthy prayers. These men will be punished most severely."[10]

For those even more on the margins, Ron visits the homeless camps in order to speak, teach, and pray with those living on the streets. He loves sharing teachings like "Foxes have dens and

---

9. Stone, *Evangelism after Christendom*, 262.

10. Luke 20:46–47, NIV.

birds have nests, but the Son of Man has no place to lay his head."[11] Ron describes the people on the street nodding along, saying, "Jesus knows what we're going through." For all of us, catechesis is an ongoing, lifelong renunciation of those promises and powers in the world that seek to lead us to death, and a call to return to the One who is the bread of life. Bryan Stone notes that one of the reasons conversion is a matter of formation over time is "that it is not simply a decision or an experience, but the acquisition of a way of life that is embodied and passed along in community."[12]

This catechetical formation is challenging work, as it unsettles those who have been comfortable in church with a more transactional or consumer-of-religion mindset. Rev. Elizabeth Ingram Schindler of Faith United Methodist Church on the outskirts of Seattle noted that in her wealthy suburban context she has found that systemic sins are easier to name than personal sin. She asks, "What does that mean for forming disciples if they are okay with using the language of social justice regarding corporate sin/structures but struggle to be honest about personal sin?" From the downtown streets of Portland to the leafy green Microsoft suburbs of Seattle and across Cascadia, churches are recognizing that how we form and equip disciples for their witness when we are not together in worship is essential. If we have lost our ability to speak about God in Christ by the time we reach coffee hour, we're in trouble, and so is the church. Post-Christendom demands that Christians are able to discern the presence of the triune God at work in their everyday lives, and when prompted to give an account of the hope that is within them, without being a jerk.[13] What that looks like is not yet clear, but the missionally minded churches of Cascadia have it on their radar. And we can't wait to find out.

---

11. Matt 8:20, NIV.

12. Stone, *Evangelism after Christendom*, 259.

13. 1 Pet 3:15.

Questions for Reflection and Reflection

1. What were the most effective ways you were formed in community for discipleship to Jesus over the years?
2. What are the particular challenges of Christian education and formation in your church and context for ministry today?
3. Where have you grown comfortable or stagnant in your apprenticeship to Jesus and what catechetical skills, tools, or training do you desire?

8

The End of the World as We Know It

Upon this writing it is too early to take lasting lessons from the year of COVID-19. (Will it just be a year? What will the final cost be in lives and treasure? Hard to judge a story without its last chapter.) But from where you are reading, some conclusions are likely starting to coalesce. One is that this was a moment of apocalypse. Not the destruction of the whole world. The virus has not killed all of us (yet!), though for grieving families and frontline health workers in hard-hit places it must feel that way. In the etymological sense, the sense Christians have been trying to recover from the Bible amidst great resistance from both fundamentalists and Hollywood, the apocalypse is the unveiling of what really is—the peeling back of the superficial to reveal the way things actually are. When Saint John sat (in great social isolation!) on the isle of Patmos, he saw a vision of Jesus Christ's reign over all things (Rev 1:10). It is not a reign like Caesar's, built on violence, premised on fear. That's the reign of the beast, the dragon, all designed to make people cower in obsequience. Instead, John sees the reign of a slain Lamb (Rev 5:6). The crucified One brings a new creation intended for the healing of the nations (Rev 22:2). When Christians say "the end is near," we're not just playing the wild-eyed zealot on the corner with the sandwich board (though there may be a place for that). We are saying that history is more than just one damn thing after another, more than just paying off the credit-card minimum and worrying why the kids don't call. History is headed somewhere: a fiery judgment that burns away our impurities and burnishes all that is lovely. The result will be the city of God, full of nothing but worship of the Lamb and love for one another (Rev 21:2).

Sign us up for that sandwich board. The end is near: no need to be afraid.

The churches in our study have figured out how to evaluate themselves on a different timeline than most social-benefit organizations, governments, businesses, or even churches. One mistaken timeline of judgment for innovative congregations can be the calling to "save our denomination." The numbers are dire. The need for a new way of operating is patent. Get your best, youngest, hippest ministers equipped to turn the ship around. The problem is it cannot be turned around. The mainline's coming "death tsunami" cannot be averted.[1] The only question is what the church will look like when it emerges from the catacombs to come. Andy Goebel of Portsmouth Union Church in Portland uses some of the harshest language we have heard to describe Christendom: it is a "carcass." No revival coming here—to a corpse. But new things grow out of carcasses. Some of the grandest trees in this region grow out of the stumps of Western Red Cedars cut down in logging operations more than a century ago. Those cedars' stumps are carcasses, birthing new life. One friend tells a story of a beached whale on one of the islands off of Cascadia's coast where hippie retirees flock to retire. The long gray ponytails came out, trying, and failing, to roll the beached creature back to the sea. Meanwhile, another group, moving with much less urgency, also took to the beach. The local indigenous tribe had long known what to do when a whale beaches. They brought out long tables and knives and sharpeners and waited. That critter would feed hundreds—let us know when you're

---

1. The language comes from Weems, *Focus*, 7 and often.

exhausted, okay, hippie neighbors? Carcasses are not to be feared. They are signs of new life.

In our interview with the leaders of Portsmouth Union, Goebel brings up the much-loved admonition from the poet Wendell Berry: "Plant sequoias." Then he chops down that thousand-year-old tree. Berry is advising patience rather than the frantic and death-dealing timetable of the market. But PUC is not trying to be a sequoia—to grow hundreds of feet over thousands of years. "Nah, this is for a season," Goebel said. "It's no failure if it ends. This is for a time and place." If you're trying to build a sequoia, you probably do not give away a chunk of your building and property for housing for those who cannot ever pay. But because PUC sees a new creation coming where the poor are blessed, it can hold its own existence lightly, and fight for its needier neighbors, rather than claw to stay open at all costs. Goebel and his fellow pastor Jules Nielsen tell us of another church nearby that PUC approached to help partner to offer housing. It became clear this church intends to sell off bits of its property at market value so it can fund doing ministry the way it has always done for as long as possible. But a vision of the coming city of God helps the church not to hoard, but to give its treasure away. Christians aren't bad at preaching against a consumerism that says a proper "no" to the bumper sticker, "He who dies with the most toys wins." That's fine for individuals. But we act like congregations should play the miser and the spendthrift in the name of longevity. Then we wonder why our neighbors don't want to have anything to do with us.

Elizabeth Ingram Schindler at Faith Church in Issaquah sees the contradictions in Cascadia vividly. Her suburban Seattle community swims in a sea of wealth, but many people feel impoverished. Folks are singularly focused on their success, their wealth, their achievement, their kids' college prospects, yet often think of themselves as "progressive." "We tend to wallpaper over brokenness," she says of American culture generally, her patch of earth in particular. But there is a high price to privilege, she says. One student in the community overdosed on Fentanyl last fall. Churches came together and memorialized well—that's what we do. But if "privilege" were the same thing as "blessing," no one would be seeking to escape through drug abuse. But check the numbers. Many are.

Ministering in an area that confuses "privilege" with "blessing" does hamper the church's work. Folks are at their jobs eighty hours a week. Gifted lay leaders have little time left over to give to their families or themselves, let alone their church. Those that escape the time crunch, as soon as they're in a position to lead well, move on to the next "opportunity." And of course, these fiscal and temporal pressures directly affect the church's budget. Staffers make what looks like exorbitant salaries on paper but have to drive an hour each way to afford housing.

What's the answer?

More intensive discipleship, Elizabeth thinks. She knows what it's like to try to hustle your way to success. She has done that as a pastor. She's well-trained theologically, fantastic at the microphone, funny and charming, heck, she even plays a mean guitar. She is adept at analyzing power dynamics—aware she is in a church of retired former CEOs who tell her she's the CEO and then tell her how to do her job. There is a reason she was sent to a church with a reputation for "eating ministers alive," and only being led by end-of-career graybeards, when she was all of thirty-three years old and, well, female. She's got gifts to spare. And yet, "God has to help me to be faithful here," she says. "I've done lots of work with a spiritual director and therapists, that's all I can do, while trusting the Spirit. I tried to *make* it thrive here, and then backed off, asking how to lead reasonably without burning out."

A proper sense of the calendar helps Ken Evers-Hood at Tualatin Presbyterian, back in Portland. Churches are adept at giving the *impression* that nothing changes. Mainline churches especially become addicted to the form with which they do things: robes and pews and church paraphernalia. Pastors know many of these "traditions" are post-World War II innovations, but we act like they are unchanging since the time of Adam. What if our sturdy frame as a mainline church became, instead, a trustworthy place from which to innovate? "We are trying to build a culture of permission here," Ken says. "You can do anything once." One tried and true mainline trick for killing innovation is tying it up in committees, like

Congress trying to pass a bill. The rules are different at Tualatin. Lay people don't have to ask permission of the church's session to try something. They need only come to the session if applying for church money or if they need help sorting out a problem. Church folks can operate relatively independently then. Ken asks them to do "what lights them up." It's their church, after all, not his, not the denomination's. "I often tell them, 'It's your church. I'm just the pastor.'" The goal is to have the congregation be an incubator for interesting failures. "Try it and see, please, we'll learn from whatever happens."

That culture of freedom and innovation applies to Tualatin's worship space as well. Ken is willing to use the space for things that, indeed, shock some. For example, for a preaching series on doors and thresholds, the church hung up a dozen or so doors in the ceiling of the sanctuary. No permission sought; no committee hurdles cleared. Folks came to church one Sunday and there the doors were. Many hated them. Ken had words of reassurance: "Don't worry, it's not permanent." Those words, which we might say over *any human endeavor*, clear space for the church to experiment. "Some were against the doors, some loved the doors, *but they made me come alive*." As Ken often says, quoting a mentor, "Interested people are interesting." Experiment away. Reassure the pearl clutchers that it'll only be there for a month. And then try anything. In the mainline, even in Cascadia, Ken believes we revert to being careful, cautious, protecting against loss. But God is always doing a new thing. He can't stand to be bored. And what brings Ken alive as a leader will be a blessing to the congregation. Not only him—but that culture of permission extends out into lay leadership as far as possible. Get busy failing, church. There is, after all, only one failure that matters. Christ's cross. And what did God do with that?

Rene and James B. Notkin learned a lot at University Presbyterian in Seattle. It is a flagship church in the region for a reason: incubating new ideas, fostering creative discipleship, the works. They often pass on theological nuggets of wisdom from former greats like Earl Palmer and Bruce Larson: Jesus never called the world to the church, rather Jesus calls the church to the world. That's good! It'll preach! It has the virtue of being biblical! And, for our purposes, missional. Faith is an adventure, a daring expedition—it is no safe course. And church in Seattle is a grander adventure still. Most cities are either financial or medical or technological or education or industry hubs (if they're lucky). Seattle has all of those. The church can then be a witness across the city. Ministry is about giving away power, disavowing ego. If we are really forgiven, let's take some risks, and see what God can do through us.

Sounds appealing, right?

The Notkins came through campus ministry with a Young Life flavor—a belief that God is pursuing every young person and asking them to influence their sphere of life for Christ. Yet that increasingly pulled them away from the model of church even in as dynamic a place as University Presbyterian Church. At the church's 100th anniversary, a massive overhaul of the campus was taking place. The Notkins put in a pitch for UPC to also fund several church plants—perhaps half a dozen? Only one came through—Union Church. Theirs would be a church in and for a neighborhood, knowing individuals by name and face, caring for the poor on a particular corner, serving gourmet chocolate and hosting local organizations as a venue space. Union Church doesn't even have a sign out front. Think of that for a moment. That would have been as unthinkable in the age of attractional church as having no website would be in ours. Union isn't trying to grow big. "We're banking on God being faithful, and that folks will discover that. That's over against an effort to market Jesus." The Notkins' vision of the kingdom, nurtured at University Presbyterian Church, birthed a very different sort of church, in line with how they view the coming kingdom.

Grandview Church in Vancouver should not exist anymore. Other churches built in the same early twentieth-century era for neighborhoods are now either pubs or cultural centers or condos. Grandview was well on its way to a similar fate when Tim Dickau arrived thirty years ago. The congregation had quit, but not told him. Garbage was piled in Sunday School rooms. The end was nigh. Tim and Mary Dickau got busy being church in the neighborhood. They had hundreds of people over for meals and had dozens of people live with them for longer periods of time. Grandview took what it had—lots of older people—and paired them with new, inexperienced young mums: "They loved those young women to bits," Tim says. Grandview established ministries to bless its neighborhood with housing for those who couldn't afford it, with refugee relief, with work opportunities, with the arts. Tim remembers reading that it takes a good ten years for a congregation to get healthy, and thinking, "Nah, we'll do it faster than that." At year ten, he looked back and saw that what he'd read had been correct. Church turnaround stories should not be told as flash paper miracles. They are miracles, but they happen in slow motion.

Much of Tim's preaching centered on the kingdom of God, and its upside-down, counterintuitive ways over against what we're peddled in the world around us. He calls it a fusion of John Perkins's civil-rights-era intentional communities in Jackson, Mississippi, with N. T. Wright's reordering of the gospel into a profoundly hopeful this-worldliness, with Ray Bakke's renewed vision for evangelical urban ministry. Grandview members started moving into neighborhood homes together to live out Christian community. They have continued as a buffer against Vancouver's crushingly high price of real estate and rentals. This cannot just be living with people who make life easy. Joy Banks, one of Dickau's successors after he stepped down at Grandview, points out that "anyone would be willing to live with their friends!" John Perkins's ministry was dedicated not only to protecting vulnerable Black people in mid-century Mississippi. He also offered love to the poor white people threatening his life. Community was the "answer" to victim and victimizer alike. Christ calls his people to live in close proximity and garden and walk to church—not just as a challenge to a world built on fossil fuels and gentrification and their attendant violence. Christ also wants us to irritate one another, forgive one another, learn how to lean into conflict and experience the peace at the far end of conflict, not the near.

Grandview has a shabby chic vibe about it. Furniture is worn, pews are creaky, the squat "steeple" looks like it needs a cross re-affixed, but no one has gotten around to it. The beauty inside and out is not stuffy. The church feels lived-in: art by the church's children and the community's professional artists, not framed relics of churchianity from prior eras. It's a place you want to settle down in and stay a while. In our interview over tea with pastor Joy Banks and her fellow pastor, Mark Glanville, he says this coziness is essential to Grandview: "This is what we do, it's how we live, it feels like family." We ask whether this metaphor for church can't be hackneyed, overused. Of course, he said. But we should have thought before we objected. Mark has a PhD in Old Testament, working on notions of kinship in ancient Judaism, and has written a recent book on the mandate to welcome the refugee in the Bible. Evangelicalism of a sort may have idealized (and idolized) the nuclear family. "But we were still made for community. That's why we all long for it. We just need it from a family in a much different form than the nuclear." In such a community, God puts us into a thick relationship with those we would not have chosen, but in fact would have excluded—the widow, the poor, the orphan, the stranger. And God asks us to find our salvation precisely there, with them—not only with Jesus, but also with all his weird friends.

Many of Grandview's people are refugees from forms of evangelicalism with thinner notions of church and salvation—a place to get individuals saved on their way to heaven. As Wright's work has shown, the Bible's vision is of a rapture in reverse: God is coming to earth, renewing his creation, not beaming believers out of it and leaving behind only destruction. When Grandview offers a place of respite as in its Stillpointe ministry of spiritual direction, or when it offers theater to a vulnerable kid through its Eastside Storyguild, it is taking part in Christ's reclamation of his creation. As Eugene Peterson once translated John's Gospel, "The Word became flesh, *and moved into the neighborhood.*"[2]

Churches often think of mission as a program, something you plan and put on the calendar and then do for other people. Grandview shows mission is the whole church's life: living in a way that is different than our neighbors *in order to bless our neighbors.* Mission is now part of Grandview's DNA. You don't move in together with people with different last names without having some serious reason. Grandview is also heady. An old soup kitchen gave rise to conversations about what we mean by words like "poverty,"

---

2. John 1:14, MSG.

"dignity," or even "food." And, as noted earlier in the book, it yield-ed a program called JustCatering, in which vulnerable people cook for their neighbors, acquire skills, grow a business, and experience the sort of dignity that a bowl of charity cannot provide. We are made for community as friends, not just to subsist and feed like functionaries.

There is a danger in this sort of church, of course (and where, gentle reader, in human endeavors, is there *not* danger?). Grandview is so all-encompassing it can wear out its leaders and members. The exhaustion comes not from programming, which Grandview is not overly keen on. It comes from being church all the time—at home, at work, in the neighborhood, at school. It is the right way to be Christian. And it is demanding. A cross. Grandview has noticed its pattern of burnout and tried to scale back its work for the next year, to practice sabbath, "to come to a full stop at the stop sign, not just a rolling stop," as one lay leader told us. To live in the kingdom way makes for life.[3] And it can make for tired legs. In one way, we need fifty more Grandview churches in Vancouver, one or more in every neighborhood. In another, one can see why folks settle for less demanding forms of church, with more religious consumerism and less kitchen table conversation. George Bernard Shaw said of socialism once, "It's a good idea, but who could stand all the meetings?" The same could be asked of the church of Jesus Christ, especially in incarnations like Grandview. We need more of them. But who could stand it?

Several of the pastors we interviewed had similar experiences with burnout. These are gifted leaders. They could try, through sheer force of will, to turn their ship around and build a thriving congregation—yet it might come at the cost of their health and wellness and those of their families. Tim Dickau at Grandview re-lates something similar. So too do Al Chu at Tapestry and Ken Shi-gematsu at Tenth. Father Matthew Tate at Annunciation Orthodox outside Portland went into his learning of this painful lesson in the most detail. He had thrown himself into his new ministry, and it had worked. The church had grown, and he had been praised. One

3. The language is Dickau's from his *Plunging Into the Kingdom Way.*

can see why—he is not only articulate and charismatic; he is flat out *handsome*—blue eyes and ponytail and the works (to go with all that Orthodox finery). "I *felt* that success. I thought I was doing it. And I kind of was, but it was not healthy. I had to learn who was really in charge." A controversy erupted that involved children harming one another and lawyers and lawsuits. The parish halved in no time. "Every phone call was someone leaving or dropping a job." Matthew found himself on the church's floor before the altar, sobbing and asking God, "What do you want?" And he heard an answer in his conscience: "Don't take credit for the good things, then you don't have to take the credit for the bad things. You just work here. They're my people, not yours." In good, Orthodox fashion, Matthew heard that his main means of healing was the sacramental life of the church—"That whole thing about fixing people and being charming is bull, so stop it." And he did. He cut down on counseling relationships, especially those with any hints of co-dependency, or if the person was not getting better. The legal issues resulted in a set of dropped lawsuits and Matthew sought resolution with all parties, finding it with all but one family. "That was the making of me," Father Matthew says. "Children suffered for it, and I wish it were otherwise." He pauses and reflects on a lesson from a ninety-four-year-old fellow priest: "You just have to let go of all this, and let it go the way it goes. If the church falls apart, let it." It's God's church. He's just the priest.

That was a cross-shaped, costly way of learning missional ministry. Father Matthew had tried an easier route—going to conferences and learning the tricks of church growth: "The most important things are adequate parking, pleasant greeters, an upbeat sermon. I laughed at the time. But it's true!" He contrasts this with, say, Origen of Alexandria in the ancient church: "he preached scary sermons!" Yet Annunciation has learned to work hard on its greeting practices, inviting people to lunch after, helping newcomers with the library of necessary books as they stand for liturgies far longer than most of us are used to. And his homilies try never to leave hearers without hope. Yet the church's mission is clearly no cheap trick. It is a cross, and only then resurrection.

Good leaders learn that cross-and-resurrection pattern. So too do congregations. There is no credit for keeping the doors from closing a little longer. Sometimes their closing is the death that precedes resurrection. Tidelands Church in western Washington started as a missional community in a living room. It took up mission, put a premium on feeding folks, threw out programming when someone new came to focus on them, and it grew. As it began looking for a permanent meeting place, pastor Brandon Bailey found a former mechanic's garage-turned-yoga-studio for sale. Digging deeper, he learned that it had once been the site of Stanwood First Presbyterian Church, which had closed in the 1920s. No one in his Presbytery had any memory of a Presbyterian Church in that part of the state. The young families in the missional communities making up Tidelands church were ready for the next step of moving into a building for Sunday worship, but they didn't have enough money. That's when the Northwest Coast Presbytery offered up funding from another Presbyterian church in the state that had just closed. At their end, the dying church asked that proceeds of the sale be used to plant another church, anywhere in the state, as an act of generous, resurrection faith. With that money from a Presbyterian church they didn't know, Bailey and Tidelands bought the property, returning a worshiping and witnessing community to a site where a hundred years earlier people had sung their last hymn and turned out the lights. A glimpse of the future hope that God intends for all creation is unveiled as being both here, *and* still to come.

That's the Christian gospel. It's precisely through death that resurrection comes. Only sometimes it takes a bit longer than three days. In that long meantime, our best theology is called for. Ross speaks from his Presbyterian tradition of the sovereignty of God— the freedom that comes from not fearing outcomes that are in the hands of a good God, and so being able to take risks in ministry. As a Methodist, Jason speaks of evangelism being done in innovative ways, reaching out to the least likely. What is the church God is bringing, and how do we pivot to take part in that, rather than default to what we've "always" done?

Ron Clark does us both one better. He has made a mission out of driving suburbanite middle-class Christians, blind to our privilege, around for *his* tour of Portland. They often give him the same feedback: they had no idea there were so many poor people in Portland. They never used to notice them. But now, having had them pointed out, they see them everywhere. Neighbors.

That's eschatology or living in light of the coming end of the world: learning to see with the coming kingdom, and noticing more of Jesus all the time, so as to point him out to others.

Questions for Reflection and Action

1. What does your congregation *really* believe about the end of the world? Not its fiery destruction, but rather, what is creation really for? Toward what future is it headed? And how do we align our congregation's life aright for that coming future, now?
2. How might your congregation develop a "culture of permission," with agency given away as widely as possible, forgiveness presumed, and so creativity encouraged?
3. How does ministry in your setting seem more like a cross than a resurrection? Can you have one without the other?

Conclusion

Treasure Map

A s we draw this project to a close, we now pass the baton to you, gentle reader, wondering what your next, most faithful step will be in light of what you've discovered here. We've illustrated for you our own treasure hunt in this particular corner of North America known as Cascadia. We are aware, however, that where our treasure map led us across Portland, Seattle, and Vancouver is just beginning to scratch the surface of what God is up to in this region. What treasure remains buried in our region, and in yours, is yet to be discovered. We began this project inspired by the faithful pursuit, with a sanctified imagination, of a group of missiologists wondering what a missionary encounter with the West would look like here in North America. Their Holy Spirit–fueled curiosity has produced many publications within the Gospel and Our Culture Network, and well beyond. The resource *Treasure in Clay Jars* was an attempt to notice, name, and nurture missional characteristics within certain Christian witnessing communities across North America twenty years ago. The missiologists asked, "If you saw a missional church, what would it look like? What patterns of behavior and practice would you find there?" Our project, of more modest means, aims, and scope, endeavored to discover some key factors at work within missional communities in our Pacific Northwest region of North America.

We are grateful to the congregations and leaders who gave so generously of their time, spoke so honestly from the heart, and offered such incredible witness to what the Triune God was up to in their midst. Twenty years ago, the authors of *Treasure in Clay Jars* went on their own treasure hunt with high expectations. The treasure they sought included missional communities that were "shaped by participating in God's mission, which is to set things right in a broken, sinful world, to redeem it, and to restore it to what God has always intended for the world." They noted that missional churches "see themselves not so much sending, as being sent," and that from worship to witness to training for discipleship, missional churches let "God's mission permeate everything." Missional churches do so in order that the gap between outreach and congregational life might be bridged, since "in its life together, the church is to embody God's mission."[1] The treasure that the authors found two decades ago in *Treasure in Clay Jars* is still valuable to study today, but that treasure is no longer in the ground. To revisit those churches today we would find very different people expressing their love of God and neighbor in new ways. So too, the congregations that we studied across Cascadia have been changing even in the timeline of our project. Our treasure map created in this book has a shelf life. But that's as it should be. Therein lies the adventure. The treasure is *not* in the particular communities or the insights they offer to those of us studying or leading our own missional congregations today. The treasure is "the light of the gospel that displays the glory of Christ,"[2] and congregations, knowing they have this gift from God, live that out in their missional vocation with a shared sense of being, "caught up into God's intent for the world."[3]

The challenge now is for you to become, in Alan Roxburgh's words, a "detective of divinity" in your own context. It's time for a treasure hunt. The treasure map you develop over time through rich conversations, prayerful discernment, and an attentiveness to the movement of the Holy Spirit where you live, will look very

1. Barrett, *Treasure in Clay Jars*, x.

2. 2 Cor 4:4.

3. Hunsberger, "Discerning Missional Vocation," 36.

different than the one you hold in your hands right now. We've discerned a treasure map, for this moment, where we live that includes an emphasis on:

1. holy urgency that fuels entrepreneurial expressions of ecclesiology,
2. a fusion of evangelical and liberal theology;
3. a willingness to name, disempower, and turn away from sacred cows of tradition for the sake of partnering with what God is up to now;
4. missional leadership that is bold yet humble, shaped by the heart and mind of God;
5. churches crafted for the local context, free from competition, and reflecting the unique characteristics, needs, and gifts of a particular community;
6. metrics of effectiveness tied to the impact of God's love for neighbor rather than prestige or self-preservation;
7. deep formation through catechesis leading to thick community that no longer looks to the culture for help in making disciples; and
8. a hopeful, future-orientated faith that frees churches (and their leaders) from building ecclesiastical fiefdoms in the here and now.

There is treasure right where you read this book today. Look around you. Look inside you. Our treasure map, for as much fun as it was creating, can only take you so far. It's time for you to start making your own. Of course, you're never really on your own in this work, right? Look, God is already on the move. A pillar of cloud by day and a pillar of fire by night. Moving forward—calling, redeeming, reconciling, and healing humanity and all creation. The ground all around you is saturated with God's prevenient (or as one of us might say "common") grace. It's time to get up and follow. A treasure hunt awaits. Just remember in all that you are about to experience, "we have this treasure in jars of clay, to show that the surpassing power belongs to God and not to us."[4]

4. 2 Cor 4:7.

Bibliography

Airhart, Phyllis. *A Church with the Soul of a Nation: Making and Remaking of The United Church of Canada.* Montreal/Kingston: McGill-Queen's University Press, 2013.

Balmer, Richard. *The Making of Evangelicalism: From Revivalism to Politics and Beyond.* Waco: Baylor University, 2017.

Barrett, Lois, ed. *Treasure in Clay Jars: Patterns in Missional Faithfulness.* Grand Rapids: Eerdmans, 2004.

Berton, Pierre. *The Comfortable Pew: A Critical Look at the Church in the New Age.* Toronto: McClelland and Stewart, 1965.

Block, Tina. *The Secular Northwest: Religion and Irreligion in Everyday Postwar Life.* Vancouver: University of British Columbia Press, 2016.

Bosch, David. *Transforming Mission: Paradigm Shifts in Theology of Mission.* Maryknoll: Orbis, 1991.

Bruenig, Elizabeth. "The Failure of Macho Christianity." *The New Republic,* February 24, 2015. https://newrepublic.com/article/121138/mark-driscoll -and-macho-christianity.

Calvin, John. *The Epistles of Paul the Apostle to the Galatians, Ephesians, Philippians and Colossians.* Calvin's New Testament Commentaries 11. Edited by David W. Torrance and Thomas F. Torrance. Grand Rapids: Eerdmans, 1965.

Clark, Ron. *The God of Second Chances: Finding Hope through the Prophets of Exile.* Eugene, OR: Cascade, 2012.

Clarke, Brian, and Stuart Macdonald. *Leaving Christianity: Changing Allegiances in Canada since 1945.* Montreal: McGill-Queens University Press, 2017.

Clements, Rob, and Dennis Ngien, eds. *Between the Lectern and Pulpit: Essays in Honour of Victor A. Shepherd.* Vancouver: Regent College Publishing, 2014.

Daniel, Lillian. *Tell It Like It Is: Reclaiming the Practice of Testimony.* Lanham, MD: Rowman & Littlefield, 2005.

Bibliography

Dickau, Tim. *Plunging into the Kingdom Way: Practicing the Shared Strokes of Community, Hospitality, Justice, and Confession.* Eugene, OR: Cascade, 2011.

Duckworth, Jessica. *Wide Welcome: How the Unsettling Presence of Newcomers Can Save the Church.* Minneapolis: Fortress, 2013.

Everts, Don, et al. *Breaking the Huddle: How Your Community Can Grow Its Witness.* Downers Grove, IL: InterVarsity, 2016.

Fitch, David. *Faithful Presence: Seven Disciplines That Shape the Church for Mission.* Downers Grove, IL: InterVarsity, 2016.

Goertz, Donald. "Toward a Missional Theology of Worship." In *Between the Lectern and Pulpit: Essays in Honour of Victor A. Shepherd,* edited by Rob Clements and Dennis Ngien, 151–72. Vancouver: Regent College Publishing, 2014.

Guder, Darrell. *Be My Witnesses: The Church's Mission, Message, and Messengers.* Grand Rapids: Eerdmans, 1985.

———. *Called to Witness: Doing Missional Theology.* Grand Rapids: Eerdmans, 2015.

———. *The Continuing Conversion of the Church.* Grand Rapids: Eerdmans, 2000.

———. "From Mission and Theology to Missional Theology." *The Princeton Seminary Bulletin* 24 (2003) 36–54.

Guder, Darrell, ed. *Missional Church: A Vision for the Sending of the Church in North America.* Grand Rapids: Eerdmans, 1998.

Hunsberger, George R. "Discerning Missional Vocation." In *Treasure in Clay Jars,* edited by Lois Barrett, 33–58. Grand Rapids: Eerdmans, 2004.

James, Christopher B. *Church Planting in Post-Christian Soil: Theology and Practice.* Oxford: Oxford University Press, 2017.

Killen, Patricia O'Connell. "Introduction." In *Religion and Public Life in the Pacific Northwest: The None Zone,* edited by Patricia O'Connell Killen and Mark Silk, 9–20. Walnut Creek, CA: Altamira, 2004.

Killen, Patricia O'Connell, and Mark Silk. *Religion and Public Life in the Pacific Northwest: The None Zone.* Walnut Creek, CA: Altamira, 2004.

Krabill, James R., and Stuart Murray, eds. *Forming Christian Habits in Post-Christendom: The Legacy of Alan and Eleanor Kreider.* Harrisonburg, VA: Herald, 2011.

Kreider, Alan. *The Patient Ferment of the Early Church: The Improbable Rise of Christianity in the Roman Empire.* Grand Rapids: Eerdmans, 2016.

Laytham, D. Brent, ed. *God Does Not . . . Entertain, Play "Matchmaker," Hurry, Demand Blood, Cure Every Illness.* Grand Rapids: Brazos, 2009.

Mancini, Will. *Church Unique: How Missional Leaders Cast Vision, Capture Culture, and Create a Movement.* San Francisco: Jossey-Bass, 2008.

Marks, Lynn. *Infidels and the Damn Churches: Irreligion and Religion in Settler British Columbia.* Vancouver: University of British Columbia Press, 2017.

Newbigin, Lesslie. "The Theory of Cross-Cultural Mission and the Ideology of Pluralism." http://commons.ptsem.edu/id/04133#audio-player-container.

Oleksa, Michael. *Orthodox Alaska: A Theology of Mission.* Crestwood, NY: St. Vladimir's Seminary Press, 1993.

Bibliography

Osmer, Richard. *The Teaching Ministry of Congregations*. Louisville: Westminster John Knox, 2005.

Paas, Stefan. *Priest and Pilgrims: Christian Mission in a Post-Christian Society*. London: SCM, 2019.

Purves, Andrew. *Crucifixion of Ministry: Surrendering Our Ambitions to the Service of Christ*. Downers Grove, IL: InterVarsity, 2007.

Roxburgh, Alan J. *Missional: Joining God in the Neighborhood*. Grand Rapids: Baker, 2011.

Roxburgh, Alan J., and Martin Robinson. *Practices for the Refounding of God's People: The Missional Challenge of the West*. London: Church, 2018.

Shigematsu, Ken. *God in My Everything: How an Ancient Rhythm Helps Busy People Enjoy God*. Grand Rapids: Zondervan, 2013.

Stone, Bryan P. *Evangelism after Christendom: The Theology and Practice of Christian Witness*. Grand Rapids: Brazos, 2006.

Todd, Douglas. "The Climate Is Changing. And So Is the Catholic Church." *The Vancouver Sun*, October 23, 2015. https://vancouversun.com/news/staff-blogs/the-climate-is-changing-and-so-is-the-catholic-church/.

———. "Health Authority Ignores Research: Fires Spiritual Care Directors." *Vancouver Sun*, December 21, 2009. https://vancouversun.com/news/staff-blogs/health-authority-ignores-research-fires-spiritual-care-directors/.

"Unique Affordable Rental Housing Project Opens in Vancouver." *Canadian Apartment Magazine*, August 28, 2018. https://www.reminetwork.com/articles/unique-affordable-rental-housing-project-opens-vancouver/.

Weems, Lovett. *Focus: The Real Challenges That Face the United Methodist Church*. Nashville: Abingdon, 2012.

Wells, Samuel. *A Nazareth Manifesto: Being With God*. Oxford: Wiley-Blackwell, 2015.